Number 152
Winter 2016

New Directions for Evaluation

Paul R. Brandon
Editor-in-Chief

Social Experiments in Practice: The What, Why, When, Where, and How of Experimental Design & Analysis

Laura R. Peck
Editor

Social Experiments in Practice: The What, Why, When, Where, and How of Experimental Design & Analysis
Laura R. Peck (ed.)
New Directions for Evaluation, no. 152
Editor-in-Chief: *Paul R. Brandon*

New Directions for Evaluation, (ISSN 1097-6736; Online ISSN: 1534-875X), is published quarterly on behalf of the American Evaluation Association by Wiley Subscription Services, Inc., a Wiley Company, 111 River St., Hoboken, NJ 07030-5774 USA.
Postmaster: Send all address changes to *New Directions for Evaluation*, John Wiley & Sons Inc., C/O The Sheridan Press, PO Box 465, Hanover, PA 17331 USA.

Information for subscribers
New Directions for Evaluation is published in 4 issues per year. Institutional subscription prices for 2017 are:
Print & Online: US$484 (US), US$538 (Canada & Mexico), US$584 (Rest of World), €381 (Europe), £304 (UK). Prices are exclusive of tax. Asia-Pacific GST, Canadian GST/HST and European VAT will be applied at the appropriate rates. For more information on current tax rates, please go to www.wileyonlinelibrary.com/tax-vat. The price includes online access to the current and all online backfiles to January 1st 2013, where available. For other pricing options, including access information and terms and conditions, please visit www.wileyonlinelibrary.com/access.

Delivery Terms and Legal Title
Where the subscription price includes print issues and delivery is to the recipient's address, delivery terms are **Delivered at Place (DAP)**; the recipient is responsible for paying any import duty or taxes. Title to all issues transfers FOB our shipping point, freight prepaid. We will endeavour to fulfil claims for missing or damaged copies within six months of publication, within our reasonable discretion and subject to availability.

Back issues: Single issues from current and recent volumes are available at the current single issue price from cs-journals@wiley.com.

Disclaimer
The Publisher, the American Evaluation Association and Editors cannot be held responsible for errors or any consequences arising from the use of information contained in this journal; the views and opinions expressed do not necessarily reflect those of the Publisher, the American Evaluation Association and Editors, neither does the publication of advertisements constitute any endorsement by the Publisher, the American Evaluation Association and Editors of the products advertised.

Publisher: New Directions for Evaluation is published by Wiley Periodicals, Inc., 350 Main St., Malden, MA 02148-5020.

Journal Customer Services: For ordering information, claims and any enquiry concerning your journal subscription please go to www.wileycustomerhelp.com/ask or contact your nearest office.
Americas: Email: cs-journals@wiley.com; Tel: +1 781 388 8598 or +1 800 835 6770 (toll free in the USA & Canada).
Europe, Middle East and Africa: Email: cs-journals@wiley.com; Tel: +44 (0) 1865 778315.
Asia Pacific: Email: cs-journals@wiley.com; Tel: +65 6511 8000.
Japan: For Japanese speaking support, Email: cs-japan@wiley.com.
Visit our Online Customer Help available in 7 languages at www.wileycustomerhelp.com/ask

Production Editor: Meghanjali Singh (email: mesingh@wiley.com).

Wiley's Corporate Citizenship initiative seeks to address the environmental, social, economic, and ethical challenges faced in our business and which are important to our diverse stakeholder groups. Since launching the initiative, we have focused on sharing our content with those in need, enhancing community philanthropy, reducing our carbon impact, creating global guidelines and best practices for paper use, establishing a vendor code of ethics, and engaging our colleagues and other stakeholders in our efforts. Follow our progress at www.wiley.com/go/citizenship

View this journal online at wileyonlinelibrary.com/journal/ev

Wiley is a founding member of the UN-backed HINARI, AGORA, and OARE initiatives. They are now collectively known as Research4Life, making online scientific content available free or at nominal cost to researchers in developing countries. Please visit Wiley's Content Access - Corporate Citizenship site: http://www.wiley.com/WileyCDA/Section/id-390082.html

Printed in the USA by The Sheridan Group.

Address for Editorial Correspondence: Editor-in-chief, Paul R. Brandon, New Directions for Evaluation, Email: brandon@hawaii.edu

Abstracting and Indexing Services
The Journal is indexed by Academic Search Alumni Edition (EBSCO Publishing); Education Research Complete (EBSCO Publishing); Higher Education Abstracts (Claremont Graduate University); SCOPUS (Elsevier); Social Services Abstracts (ProQuest); Sociological Abstracts (ProQuest); Worldwide Political Sciences Abstracts (ProQuest).

Cover design: Wiley
Cover Images: © Lava 4 images | Shutterstock

For submission instructions, subscription and all other information visit:
wileyonlinelibrary.com/journal/ev

Editorial Policy and Procedures

New Directions for Evaluation, a quarterly sourcebook, is an official publication of the American Evaluation Association. The journal publishes works on all aspects of evaluation, with an emphasis on presenting timely and thoughtful reflections on leading-edge issues of evaluation theory, practice, methods, the profession, and the organizational, cultural, and societal context within which evaluation occurs. Each issue of the journal is devoted to a single topic, with contributions solicited, organized, reviewed, and edited by one or more guest editors.

The editor-in-chief is seeking proposals for journal issues from around the globe about topics new to the journal (although topics discussed in the past can be revisited). A diversity of perspectives and creative bridges between evaluation and other disciplines, as well as chapters reporting original empirical research on evaluation, are encouraged. A wide range of topics and substantive domains are appropriate for publication, including evaluative endeavors other than program evaluation; however, the proposed topic must be of interest to a broad evaluation audience.

Journal issues may take any of several forms. Typically they are presented as a series of related chapters, but they might also be presented as a debate; an account, with critique and commentary, of an exemplary evaluation; a feature-length article followed by brief critical commentaries; or perhaps another form proposed by guest editors.

Submitted proposals must follow the format found via the Association's website at http://www.eval.org/Publications/NDE.asp. Proposals are sent to members of the journal's Editorial Advisory Board and to relevant substantive experts for single-blind peer review. The process may result in acceptance, a recommendation to revise and resubmit, or rejection. The journal does not consider or publish unsolicited single manuscripts.

Before submitting proposals, all parties are asked to contact the editor-in-chief, who is committed to working constructively with potential guest editors to help them develop acceptable proposals. For additional information about the journal, see the "Statement of the Editor-in-Chief" in the Spring 2013 issue (No. 137).

Paul R. Brandon, Editor-in-Chief
University of Hawai'i at Mānoa
College of Education
1776 University Avenue
Castle Memorial Hall, Rm. 118
Honolulu, HI 968222463
e-mail: nde@eval.org

Acknowledgments

The writing of several chapters in this issue was supported, in part, by the Laura and John Arnold Foundation, which had no editorial influence or control over the content. The authors are grateful for useful input from six anonymous reviewers and the editor of *New Directions for Evaluation*. In addition to receiving editorial review, selected chapters were reviewed by Stephen Bell and Howard Rolston of Abt Associates Inc., Howard White of the Campbell Collaboration, and Austin Nichols of the DeBruce Foundation's Institute for Upward Mobility. Anne Kelleher and Jan Nicholson provided editorial and production assistance.

Contents

EDITOR'S NOTES

SOCIAL EXPERIMENTS IN PRACTICE: INTRODUCTION, FRAMING, AND CONTEXT

Randomized experiments are a central tool for learning about and improving social policies and programs. With an extensive amount of practice to draw on, evaluators are improving the flexibility of experimental studies to permit their wider use as appropriate.

At times contentious debate has undermined constructive discussions about evaluation methods suited to assessing the causal impacts of policies and programs. One recent example followed the U.S. Department of Education's Institute for Education Sciences' (IES) 2003 statement declaring a preference for experiments in educational evaluations. In response to the IES statement, some members of the American Evaluation Association (AEA) declared that "we do not agree that 'evaluation methods using an experimental design are best for determining project effectiveness'" (AEA, 2003, para. 8). In a rebuttal to that position, a noted scholar proclaimed that "the AEA now has the same relationship to the Field of Evaluation as the Flat Earth Society has to the Field of Geology" (Donaldson & Christie, 2005, p. 71). In line with the AEA members' initial comment, the National Education Association (NEA) echoed that "other rigorous, equally useful evaluation methods of an intervention's effectiveness" should be allowed under the IES guidelines (NEA, 2003, p. 2).

In order to bring some evidence to bear on this debate about evidence, a number of "replication" studies have compared results from nonexperimental evaluations with results from experimental evaluations. The earliest social policy replication studies (e.g., Fraker & Maynard, 1987; LaLonde, 1986) reached pessimistic conclusions, with their quasiexperimental analyses supporting different conclusions than the experimental evidence suggested. Glazerman, Levy, and Myers (2003) summarize this literature as of that time. As the field has evolved, alternative nonexperimental methods have in some cases replicated the results from their matched experiments, at least in terms of the direction if not the magnitude of impact estimates (e.g., Cook, Shadish, & Wong, 2008; Cook, Steiner, & Pohl, 2008; Pohl et al., 2009; Shadish, 2011; St. Clair, Cook, & Hallberg, 2014). To date, roughly 30 of these social policy evaluation replication studies have been undertaken. The field is beginning to amass both evidence and theory to understand which circumstances permit specific nonexperimental designs to provide solid causal evidence of policy or program effects (Cook, 2013).

NEW DIRECTIONS FOR EVALUATION, no. 152, Winter 2016 © 2016 Wiley Periodicals, Inc., and the American Evaluation Association. Published online in Wiley Online Library (wileyonlinelibrary.com) • DOI: 10.1002/ev.20215

We laud this progress but do not intend to enter the debate about nonexperimental vs. experimental designs. Moreover, although we recognize that there are other important policy questions besides those regarding impacts on the target population, these are not the focus of this special issue.[1]

Although we do not imply that they should supplant learning about or applying other impact evaluation designs or analytic approaches, or questions other than those about impacts, experimental evaluation designs and related analytic approaches are our focus. With this as introduction, this Editor's Note turns next to defining the experimental evaluation rationale and design, articulating what this special issue aims to accomplish, explaining the choice of topics and authors, and contextualizing the issues.

What Are Experiments and Why Do We Do Them?

We begin by describing the experimental approach to measuring social program impacts by using trials in the medical or pharmaceutical field as a useful and familiar introduction. To test whether a new medicine is effective, pharmaceutical researchers undertake randomized controlled trials. These trials randomly assign some people to take, for example, a new medicine, whereas others take a placebo (an inert dose). By measuring both groups' subsequent outcomes, researchers can determine not only the extent to which the drug made the intended difference (e.g., in reducing symptoms or disease) but also any unintended side effects. Because the participants are assigned at random to the two groups, the only difference in their experiences—on average—is their drug treatment, so any differences in outcomes can confidently be attributed to that treatment.

To test the effectiveness of a public policy, social program, or other intervention, researchers can use the same approach used in medicine to address social and economic ills or achieve social goals. Social experiments randomly allocate access to an intervention to create two groups whose average experiences are the same except for access to the intervention. Often one group is the "treatment group," which has access to a program or is subject to a policy, and the other group is a "control group" excluded from

---

[1] One of the most widely used evaluation textbooks—Rossi, Lipsey, and Freeman's *Evaluation: A Systematic Approach*, now in its seventh edition (2004)—suggests a hierarchy of considerations that should come into play in considering a program's merit (p. 80): (a) need for the program, as concerns a social ill that should be addressed, (b) persuasiveness of the program design in theory and based on past evidence, (c) success of the program's process and implementation, (d) program outcomes/impact, and (e) program cost and efficiency in achieving those results. The first three steps in the hierarchy are not about program impact but about program motivation and operations, and for these purposes, the question of a valid counterfactual does not arise. This issue centers on the fourth goal of the hierarchy—achieving program impacts—and on one particular methodology for measuring that achievement—a randomized experiment.

NEW DIRECTIONS FOR EVALUATION • DOI: 10.1002/ev

the program or policy for research purposes. In other cases, two or more groups are assigned to different interventions.

This "coin toss" to allocate access to treatment carries substantial power. It allows us to rule out alternative explanations for differences in the outcomes between people who have access to a service and people who do not. Unless we engineer the underlying equivalence of the two groups in this way, comparisons between participants and nonparticipants are likely to reflect many other influences in addition to any effect of the service itself. For example, those who volunteer to participate may have better outcomes because they have greater motivation than those who do not volunteer, even if the program has no effect. Conversely, participants may self-select because of greater need and may have worse outcomes than nonparticipants even if the program actually improved participants' outcomes. Similarly, program staff can select or "cream" who gains access to their program, which implies that their outcomes will be better because of their preexisting characteristics regardless of anything the program might do for them. By providing a solid "counterfactual"—that is, data concerning what would have happened to participants in the absence of the intervention—the randomized experimental design avoids mistaking maturation, selection, and historical, political, economic, or social trends—which also influence program participants' outcomes—for effects of the program. In brief, well-executed experimentally designed evaluations support accurate identification of whether programs or policies have *caused* desired (or unanticipated) outcomes, information essential to deciding whether to expand, modify, or terminate those programs or policies. We recognize that other kinds of evaluation research are relevant to answering other kinds of questions about social policy and practice, but when it comes to the question of cause and effect—the question of a program or policy's impact—we assert that a randomized experiment should be the evaluation design of choice.

Experimental evaluations have limitations and drawbacks, including ethical, practical, scientific, and technical concerns (e.g., Bell & Peck, 2016; Blustein, 2005; Boruch, Victor, & Cecil, 2000; Greenberg & Barnow, 2014). Although it is beyond the scope of this chapter to address all of these concerns, we highlight three that are especially important because of their relevance to this issue of *New Directions for Evaluation* (NDE). First, we recognize that legal and ethical concerns sometimes preclude experiments. This is true for social experiments just as it is for medical or pharmaceutical experiments. A broad body of scholarship, tradition, law, and regulation governs research on human subjects, including social experiments (National Commission for the Protection of Human Subjects of Biomedical and Behavioral Research, 1979; U.S. Department of Health and Human Services, 2009). Another criticism of experiments is that—although they provide an unbiased, causal estimate of the effect of an intervention or policy—often they shed no light on the contribution of individual details of that intervention to its overall impact. These component impacts are often said to exist within a metaphorical "black box." The authors of the chapters of this issue examine recent innovations in experimental design and respond directly to this critique. These innovations expand the circumstances in which researchers can use experiments and gain access to the contents of the black box. Third, scholars have pointed out that the strength of experimental design for tackling challenges of internal validity has usually come at the cost of diminished external validity (e.g., Olsen, Orr, Bell, & Stuart, 2013). In other words, a design that achieves internal validity to establish a cause-and-effect relationship between program and outcome may have limited external validity, meaning that results do not readily generalize to a larger population. As elaborated in two chapters in this issue, evaluators can ease this trade-off. Indeed, experiments designed with an eye to generalizability can have strong external validity as well as internal validity. We note that (a) the *American Journal of Evaluation* volume 36, issue 4 (2015) is a special issue considering design and analytic strategies for getting inside the "black box" of experiments; and (b) at this writing, *Evaluation Review* is in the process of preparing a special issue considering external validity for randomized trials. We recommend those sources—in conjunction with this issue—for a deeper understanding of these issues and their implications for evaluation practice.

This Issue

The main purpose of this issue is to describe innovations in the design and analysis of experimental evaluations, innovations that serve to overcome previous limitations of experiments, thereby opening opportunities for their expanded use and utility. The issue's specific topics have their origins in a daylong forum titled "Social Experiments in Practice: The Why, When, Where, and How of Experimental Design & Analysis" cohosted by Abt Associates and the Association for Public Policy Analysis and Management (APPAM). Video recordings of all of the forum's presentations are available at http://tinyurl.com/AbtForum/. The organizers of the event sought out ongoing work at the methodological frontiers of experimental impact evaluation across a range of social policy areas (e.g., health, education, welfare, training, employment, and education) and sponsored by a range of federal, state, and foundation clients. To decide on the topics to include in the forum, senior methodological experts at Abt Associates convened to craft an agenda and select presenters and commentators, both from within and outside Abt. Authors for this issue include individuals involved in the forum along with some additional authors. All authors are experts in their fields and sectors and are noted scholars and practitioners whose insights provide coherence and value to this special issue.

Despite the broad objectives of the forum and the expertise of the authors, the manuscripts included in this issue of NDE do not cover all the topics related to the use and practice of social experiments. We draw primarily from studies conducted by external third-party evaluators and so do not consider methods related to, for example, participatory, empowerment, developmental, or collaborative evaluations in general. We do not deeply consider technical issues related to group or cluster designs; evaluation issues related to saturation or place-based interventions; and challenges related to the multiple comparisons inevitably made in large-scale evaluations, with many outcomes, subgroups of interest, and multiple sites to consider. Further, the content in this issue does not tackle certain topics of keen importance—such as needed improvements in administrative data availability, collection, and use—that are relevant not only to experiments but also to many other kinds of evaluations.

Before discussing the scholarly and practical context for the collection of chapters in the issue, we provide a brief discussion of how each chapter provides insights on social experiments in practice. After this chapter introduces what experiments are and their context, the chapters that follow sequentially respond to questions about why, when, where, and how social experiments are carried out in practice.

In Chapter 1, Howard Rolston considers why the use of experiments has grown so substantially in the social policy realm. He shares lessons from the past nearly 50 years of social policy experimentation. He argues that although any scientific method has limitations, the history of social policy experiments has demonstrated their utility and value and produced methods for overcoming practical barriers to their application. The expansion of the use of social experiments has involved not just greater numbers but, even more important, more diverse contexts in which evaluators apply them.

Next, Diana Epstein and Jacob Klerman discuss how to determine when a program is ready for evaluation using a randomized experiment (Chapter 2). The authors present criteria to help decision makers judge programs' readiness to pass through what they call the "impact evaluation tollgate." Expanding on Wholey's (1994) "evaluability assessment" concept, Epstein and Klerman suggest that piloting and verifying the intermediate steps of a program's logic model provide a basis for undertaking a rigorous experimental impact evaluation.

Two subsequent chapters consider the "where" question in experimental policy research, both where experiments are run and the implications of site selection for the generalizability of results. In Chapter 3, Stephen Bell and Elizabeth Stuart describe research strategies for investigating how much nonrepresentative site selection may bias impact findings. They note that the magnitude of external validity bias is potentially much larger than what we think of as an acceptable level of internal validity bias and argue that external validity bias should always be investigated by the best available means and addressed directly when presenting evaluation results. These observations flag the importance of making external validity a priority in evaluation planning. In Chapter 4, Robert Olsen and Larry Orr usefully inform this planning by making four practical recommendations to help researchers generate impact estimates that generalize to the broader population of policy interest: (a) be explicit in identifying the population to which study findings should generalize, (b) create a sampling frame that encompasses that population, (c) select a random sample—or strategically stratified random sample—of sites, and (d) use samples of sufficient size to give sharp impact inferences even with the additional "noise" that enters statistical estimates due to random sampling. They argue that following these recommendations will provide ideal conditions for establishing strong external validity from an experimental evaluation.

The next three chapters focus on various aspects of the "how" questions that social experiments can address—that is, by what means do the interventions under study achieve their impacts? In Chapter 5, Larry Mead examines the role of implementation research in learning how program operations associate with results. He argues that evaluations can contribute to the broader process of governmental learning about program and policy impact only when they include implementation research. In Chapter 6, Laura Peck discusses analyses of impacts whose nature and occurrence for a specific subset of study participants are shaped by postrandom assignment (endogenous) events or experiences. The specific analytic strategies involved build on the strength of an experimental design to help answer questions about the mediators—(i.e., postprogram-entry influences)—of program impacts. Then, building from the observation that "design trumps analysis" (Rubin, 2008), Stephen Bell and Laura Peck in Chapter 7 suggest innovative design strategies for structuring experiments to reveal what aspects of multifaceted programs generate impacts, without risk of selection and other sources of bias.

Finally, in concluding, three experienced practitioner–scholars place the work of this volume in context: Rebecca Maynard, Demetra Nightingale, and Naomi Goldstein consider the federal perspectives on the evaluation process, sharing insights about strategies for maximizing the success and utility of evaluations with careful planning and oversight.

Contextualization

The use of experimental evaluation results to guide social policy and programs appears to be on the rise. At the federal level, several recent initiatives prioritize funding for approaches with evidence of effectiveness, emphasizing experimental evidence (Haskins & Margolis, 2015). Bipartisan legislation has recently established a Commission on Evidence-Based Policymaking, which will, among other activities, "make recommendations on how best to incorporate outcomes measurement, institutionalize randomized controlled trials, and [incorporate] rigorous impact analysis into program design" (Evidence-Based Policymaking Commission Act, 2015). Organizations have begun promoting the use of evidence at the state and local levels as well, albeit with varying degrees of emphasis on experimental approaches. These trends mirror activity in the private sector (Manzi, 2012).

Drawing on Donaldson's (2007) framework for a "program theory-driven evaluation science," we connect the chapters in this issue to three stages of evaluation practice. Chapter 2 and 5 relate to the first stage, involving the development of a program impact theory, often known as a logic model or theory of change. Epstein and Klerman (Chapter 2) focus explicitly on the role of program theory and associated program implementation for providing a tollgate for a program's preparation for evaluation. Mead (Chapter 5) discusses the role of implementation research in assessing evaluability.

The second stage is formulating and prioritizing evaluation questions and aligning the evaluation design and analysis with those questions (Donaldson, 2007). Indeed, this entire issue is about connecting the most rigorous impact evaluation tools with questions that go beyond asking about the average treatment effect to focus on questions about what works. The contribution of this issue is to highlight design and analytic innovations that can help experimental evaluations address a wider range of questions than commonly thought possible. We hope that the insights of these chapters elevate evidence from experiments as fitting in many settings. That said, we recognize that some evaluation questions will demand nonexperimental designs and analytic methods; and we agree with Donaldson that the research question should be the driving force for identifying suitable designs and analyses.

Donaldson's third step is answering evaluation questions (Donaldson, 2007). Chapters 3 and 4 in this issue provide insights on how experimentally designed evaluations can produce results that are widely generalizable, improving upon their reputation of having limited external validity. Further, Chapters 5, 6, and 7 focus on answering "how" questions in experimental evaluations, specifically with attention to the role of implementation evaluation, creativity in evaluation design, and opportunities for extending analysis of experimental evaluation data to inform answers to "what works" questions.

The increased appetite for rigorous evaluation findings should raise expectations for social experiments and inspire those who design and execute them. With growing demand for the findings, evaluators more than ever must plan studies to be useful. As difficult as it is to successfully execute an experimental evaluation with rigor and integrity, social experiments must aim for more. They must generate findings that are useful and informative for decision makers. If they do not, they will disappoint—possibly undermining continued interest in this powerful tool. The chapters in this issue describe a number of ways that evaluators can enhance the usefulness of experiments by addressing some of the most persistent challenges in the field.

References

American Evaluation Association. (2003). American Evaluation Association response to U.S. Department of Education: Notice of proposed priority, Federal Register RIN 1890-ZA00. Retrieved from http://www.eval.org/p/cm/ld/fid=95

Bell, S. H., & Peck, L. R. (2016). On the feasibility of extending social experiments to wider applications. *MultiDisciplinary Journal of Evaluation*, 12(27), 93–112.

Blustein, J. (2005). Toward more public discussion of the ethics of federal social program evaluation. *Journal of Policy Analysis and Management*, 24, 824–846. doi: 10.1002/pam.20141

Boruch, R. F., Victor, T., & Cecil, J. S. (2000). Resolving ethical and legal problems in randomized experiments. *Crime & Delinquency*, 46, 330–353. doi: 10.1177/0011128700046003005

Cook, T. D. (2013). *Moving beyond existence proofs in within-study comparisons: Identifying when matching, regression-discontinuity and interrupted time series studies produce similar estimates to randomized experiments.* Presentation to the Evaluation Method Center, Abt Associates Inc., Bethesda, MD, November 29.

Cook, T. D., Shadish, W. R., & Wong, V. C. (2008). Three conditions under which experiments and observational studies produce comparable causal estimates: New findings from within-study comparisons. *Journal of Policy Analysis and Management*, 27, 724–750.

Cook, T. D., Steiner, P. M., & Pohl, S. (2008). How bias reduction is affected by covariate choice, unreliability, and mode of data analysis: Results from two types of within-study comparisons. *Multivariate Behavioral Research*, 44, 828–847.

Donaldson, S. I. (2007). *Program theory-driven evaluation science: Strategies and applications.* Mahwah, NJ: Erlbaum.

Donaldson, S. I., & Christie, C. A. (2005). The 2004 Claremont debate: Lipsey vs. Scriven—determining causality in program evaluation and applied research: Should experimental evidence be the gold standard? *Journal of Multidisciplinary Evaluation*, 3, 60–77.

Evidence-Based Policymaking Commission Act of 2015, H.R.1831, S. 991, 114th Cong. (2015). Retrieved from https://www.congress.gov/bill/114th-congress/house-bill/1831

Fraker, T., & Maynard, R. (1987). The adequacy of comparison group designs for evaluations of employment-related programs. *Journal of Human Resources*, 22, 194–227.

Glazerman, S., Levy, D. M., & Myers, D. (2003). Nonexperimental versus experimental estimates of earnings impacts. *Annals of the American Academy of Political and Social Science*, 589, 63–93.

Greenberg, D., & Barnow, B. S. (2014). Flaws in evaluations of social programs: Illustrations from randomized controlled trials. *Evaluation Review*, 38, 359–387. doi: 10.1177/0193841X14545782

Haskins, R., & Margolis, G. (2015). *Show me the evidence: Obama's fight for rigor and results in social policy.* Washington, DC: Brookings Institution.

LaLonde, R. J. (1986). Evaluating the econometric evaluations of training programs with experimental data. *American Economic Review*, 76, 604–620.

Manzi, J. (2012). *Uncontrolled: The surprising payoff of trial-and-error for business, politics, and society.* New York, NY: Basic Books.

National Commission for the Protection of Human Subjects of Biomedical and Behavioral Research. (1979). *Ethical principles and guidelines for the protection of human subjects of research (The Belmont Report).* Retrieved from http://www.hhs.gov/ohrp/humansubjects/guidance/belmont.html

National Education Association. (2003). Letter to Rod Paige. Retrieved from http://www.eval.org/d/do/51

Olsen, R. B., Orr, L. L., Bell, S. H., & Stuart, E. A. (2013). External validity in policy evaluations that choose sites purposively. *Journal of Policy Analysis and Management, 32*, 107–121. doi:10.1002/pam.21660

Pohl, S., Steiner, P. M., Eisermann, J., Soellner, R., & Cook, T. D. (2009). Unbiased causal inference from an observational study: Results of a within-study comparison. *Educational Evaluation and Policy Analysis, 31*, 463–479. doi:10.3102/0162373709343964

Rossi, P. H., Lipsey, M. W., & Freeman, H. E. (2004). *Evaluation: A systematic approach,* 7th ed. Thousand Oaks, CA: SAGE Publications.

Rubin, D. B. (2008). For objective causal inference, design trumps analysis. *Annals of Applied Statistics, 2*, 808–840.

Shadish, W. R. (2011). Randomized controlled studies and alternative designs in outcome studies challenges and opportunities. *Research on Social Work Practice, 21*, 636–643. doi:10.1177/1049731511403324

St. Clair, T., Cook, T. D., & Hallberg, K. (2014). Examining the internal validity and statistical precision of the comparative interrupted time series design by comparison with a randomized experiment. *American Journal of Evaluation.* doi: 10.1177/1098214014527337

U.S. Department of Education. (2003). Scientifically Based Evaluation Methods. *Federal Register,* Vol. 68, No. 213, RIN 1890-ZA00. Retrieved from https://www.gpo.gov/fdsys/pkg/FR-2003-11-04/pdf/03-27699.pdf

U.S. Department of Health and Human Services. (2009). *Code of Federal Regulations Title 45 Part 46: Protection of human subjects.* Retrieved from http://www.hhs.gov/ohrp/sites/default/files/ohrp/policy/ohrpregulations.pdf

Wholey, J. S. (1994). Assessing the feasibility and likely usefulness of evaluation. In J. S. Wholey, H. P. Hatry, & K. E. Newcomer (Eds.), *Handbook of practical program evaluation.* San Francisco, CA: Jossey-Bass.

Laura R. Peck Issue Editor
Naomi Goldstein

LAURA R. PECK is a principal scientist at Abt Associates Inc., Social and Economic Policy Division and director of the Research and Evaluation Expertise Center.

NAOMI GOLDSTEIN is deputy assistant secretary for planning, research and evaluation at the Administration for Children and Families, U.S. Department of Health and Human Services.

Rolston, H. (2016). On the "why" of social experiments: Some lessons on overcoming barriers from 45 years of social experiments. In L. R. Peck (Ed.), *Social experiments in practice: The what, why, when, where, and how of experimental design & analysis. New Directions for Evaluation, 152*, 19–31.

1

On the "Why" of Social Experiments: Some Lessons on Overcoming Barriers from 45 Years of Social Experiments

Howard Rolston

Abstract

Nearly a half century has passed since August 1968 when the first families were enrolled in the New Jersey Income Maintenance Experiment, the first large-scale social policy evaluation to use random assignment. Over that time, the field of social policy experiments has expanded greatly with particularly fast growth occurring since the turn of the 21st century. This dramatic growth has several dimensions, including both the volume of experiments and the numbers of areas of social policy involved. This chapter focuses on the evolving contexts in which social policy experiments have taken place, with attention to how they have overcome obstacles to their use. © 2016 Wiley Periodicals, Inc., and the American Evaluation Association.

Nearly a half century has passed since August 1968 when the first families were enrolled in the New Jersey Income Maintenance Experiment, the first large-scale social policy evaluation to use random assignment (Kershaw & Fair, 1976). Over that time, the field of social policy experiments has expanded greatly with particularly fast growth occurring since the turn of the 21st century. This dramatic growth has several dimensions, including both the volume of experiments and the numbers of areas of social policy involved. This chapter focuses on a third dimension of the expansion over the past 47 years—the contexts in which social policy experiments have addressed questions of causal effects.

Examining the various contexts of randomized experimental studies and how they have developed is important because, when successfully implemented, an experiment is the strongest method of establishing causality in the social sciences. As described in greater detail in the Editor's Note, by randomly assigning individuals either to have access to a program or policy or to a control group that does not have access, experiments unambiguously rule out, except for a quantifiable level of chance, other explanations of the effects of having this access that the experiment identifies. If impediments to experiments exist that cannot be overcome, researchers will need to rely on weaker methods, but having the most reliable findings is motivation for finding ways to overcome these impediments. Fortunately, barriers to successful social experiments have often proven to be surmountable. Researchers created new practices, many of which became routine and overcame ethical, practical, and methodological barriers. Finally, important ongoing work, much of which is reflected in other chapters in this volume, is leading to new practices and further expanding what we can learn from social experiments.

To support these claims, this chapter examines two major expansions of the contexts in which social policy experiments have been used to answer important causal questions: (a) the use of individual random assignment to evaluation in ongoing programs and (b) the use of random assignment not just of individuals but of groups of individuals or other aggregate units. No new history is recounted here. Rather the intention of describing everyday practices, and the contexts from which they evolved, is to remind readers how the practice of social science experiments has changed, as well as to illustrate how many impediments to conducting experiments have been reduced or overcome.

To aid reader understanding and to organize the discussion, this chapter relies on the terminology I describe here. The terms "impediment," "barrier," and related nouns are intended to describe conditions that render randomized trials infeasible, unethical, or methodologically problematic. Infeasibility is a broad category that includes such conditions as requiring too many individuals or places to be assigned; being too costly compared to research budgets or the value of the findings; and being unable to require participation by, or recruitment of, programs in the evaluation. Ethical barriers are those that on balance would treat human subjects inappropriately, thereby rendering the conduct of an experiment morally wrong. Methodological barriers include those that would lead to biased, unreliable findings, would not answer the research questions, or would significantly limit the utility of the findings.

Before embarking on this recounting of historical shifts, it is important to qualify the claim of this chapter. The claim is not that *all* barriers to randomized social experiments can be overcome. Some limitations of the method are inherent, such as the stable unit treatment value assumption (SUTVA is the assumption that one unit's outcomes are unaffected by another unit's treatment assignment; Rubin, 1980) and the mathematical laws of statistics. And, of course, there must be multiple instances of the units of interest that can be randomly assigned, so experiments are of no direct help in understanding, for example, unique historical events. Finally, some very deep practical limitations also abound. For example, although theoretically imaginable, one would not expect the Department of Defense to choose among several different designs of advanced strike fighters by building all of them and then testing them in a variety of randomly assigned combat situations. Within these fixed barriers, the history of social experiments suggests many other barriers can be surmounted as practice advances.

Contexts Shift: From Policy Research to Program Evaluation

The first social experiments were what are dubbed "response surface" experiments in that they attempted to estimate how behavioral responses varied with altered incentives. For example, the Income Maintenance Experiments randomly assigned families to multiple treatment conditions that varied the "guarantee" (the amount a family with no income received) and the "benefit reduction rate" (how the guarantee declined with increased earnings) of a negative income tax to determine how altering these program parameters affected the labor supply of eligible individuals. These studies were not attempts to figure out whether a particular program variant "worked" but rather to estimate behavioral responses to determine the labor supply consequences of varying the design of a negative income tax. However, by 1975 the original context, a research study, had expanded to the context of a demonstration, Supported Work, to test an actual program intervention. Although there were multiple target populations for Supported Work, unlike the response surface research projects, there was only a single intervention and, like the earlier experiments, the interventions were new rather than ongoing programs (Gueron & Rolston, 2013).

The next and most important step was to extend the use of random assignment of individuals from research and demonstration projects to the evaluation of existing programs. With this expansion to evaluation of ongoing programs operating at their intended scale, rather than at the smaller scale of research and demonstration projects, researchers faced substantial impediments to success.[1] One set of impediments arose as the result of needing to determine program eligibility for a group large enough both to fill all program slots (the treatment group) and to serve as the control group

---

[1] For the sake of brevity, this chapter addresses only experimental evaluations of ongoing programs themselves, not alternative variants of existing programs. Generally, the latter raise fewer issues (although there are some parallel barriers to evaluations of the programs themselves) than evaluations that deny access to existing programs.

(unserved by the program). That is, unlike some nonexperimental designs, recruiting more individuals than will be served is necessary for randomized experimental designs. Although this was, of course, also a requirement for the earlier research and demonstration experiments, recruitment of a group of individuals that will not be served had different implications for feasibility, ethics, and methods when applied to full-scale ongoing programs.

In the context of a new program, a lack of history implies no or few prior expectations for serving a given number of individuals. Ideally, sufficient resources would be available so that researchers could determine the size of the treatment and control groups based on a power analysis of what is necessary to detect the smallest effects of interest. However, an established program creates many more expectations, such as an expected number of individuals to be served with available resources, sufficient staff to serve that number, and a recruitment approach geared to identifying the number who will be served (and perhaps a few more to fill slots if there are no-shows or dropouts). The upshot is that, except in times of budget cutbacks when forces external to the evaluation require it, a reduction in the number served is seldom an option for most evaluations of existing programs, and overrecruitment to obtain sufficient numbers to create a control group is the most typical situation.

With respect to feasibility, in some situations, for example, in some of the welfare-to-work evaluations, thousands or tens of thousands of eligible individuals more than could be served, and whose eligibility typically could be easily determined, were available to form an adequately sized control group. However, this is seldom the case. More often, programs aim at recruiting few beyond the number they hope to serve. Marketing to, and determining eligibility for, more than the number a program typically serves costs more, and programs do not like to deny access to eligible individuals and deal with their disappointment. Having to recruit perhaps twice the number of individuals they will serve can place a substantial cost and psychic burden on programs. The cost can range from small to substantial, and if the latter is the case, then the solution to the problem can be that the evaluation funds the additional costs and also provides technical assistance on how best to increase recruitment. Addressing the psychic cost of denying program access to those in the control group also is necessary, and because program staff often expresses this cost as an ethical concern, the feasibility of experimental evaluations of existing programs is closely tied to the ethics of carrying them out.

A central principle for assessing if a social experiment is ethical and not simply feasible is that random assignment not lead to a reduction in the level of existing services (usually measured by the number of individuals served). Typically, *equipoise* about a new program—uncertainty about whether it adds to or diminishes outcomes achieved by the preexisting environment—is sufficient to deem a randomized experimental study ethical. However, most researchers and, more important, most institutional review boards, recognize that although equipoise may be necessary for conducting an experiment, it is not a sufficient justification for reducing the level of existing services where resources continue to be adequate. Perhaps this is so, because given the complexity and variety of human social environments and the lack of compelling empirically verified theory, we can always question the external validity of earlier results and find a plausible argument for equipoise: "Sure it proved itself to be effective in two previous rigorous studies but that does not necessarily mean it will be effective in *these* circumstances, for *this* population, and at *this* time." That equipoise would appear to allow the reduction of services in an existing program and permit resources that were raised to fund it to go unused suggests the addition of a stronger principal, namely that there be no service reduction.[2]

This latter principle is also central to convincing others of the ethics of randomizing as part of an evaluation. An ongoing program almost always has stakeholders with expectations—applicants for and participants in the program, funders of it, program staff, sources of program referrals, other programs that provide adjunct services to program participants, and often many others. To successfully implement a randomized evaluation requires convincing at least a subset of these stakeholders that it will be ethical to do so. For example, a program may rely on serving individuals who are referred from another program accustomed to having that program accept all its referrals. Finding out that a subset of their referrals will be in a control group will not be easy to accept. Although it will not necessarily be successful, the argument that there will be no reduction in the number served may mollify them and most other stakeholders.

Because experimental evaluations of social programs almost always require substantial recruitment beyond the number that can be served, and because programs tend to recruit just beyond the numbers they need to fill their programs, the typical evaluation requires recruiting at a higher than normal level. As a result, many more individuals will be recruited, found eligible, and then denied access to the program. This overrecruitment raises further ethical considerations. One consideration is that individuals will be

---

[2] This raises the question of whether nonreduction of existing services is also a sufficient condition for conducting an experiment. A generally accepted idea is that impact of entitlement programs should not be tested in experiments that deny benefits to those who would otherwise be legally entitled to them. (This can sometimes be legal as a result of waiver authority; see section 1115 of the Social Security Act.) The principle of nonreduction of existing services does not clearly prohibit this, because the principle is based on the level of service, not whether someone who might otherwise receive the service now will be denied (which happens in every social experiment of existing programs). One can imagine an evaluation in which, through extensive outreach, far more eligible individuals receive an entitlement benefit, but now some are denied, and this is ethically questionable. Therefore, perhaps another principle is needed. Also difficult is determining if alternative entitlement rules should be tested experimentally if they make some individuals better off and others worse off.

selected from this larger group randomly. Random selection is usually regarded as a positive feature, because lotteries are generally regarded as a fair way of allocating a limited resource. A lottery also may be a fairer selection method than a program is currently using, such as relying on family or other connections or whether an applicant is "likable." For example, it is not unusual for programs to fall into recruitment patterns that focus on certain neighborhoods or ethnic groups in their catchment areas because program staff are familiar with them. In such cases, overrecruitment induced by an experimental evaluation can have positive moral consequences insofar as it leads to a fairer distribution of the opportunity to participate in a potentially valuable program.

However, recruitment of additional individuals also has a negative aspect: because programs market by emphasizing the value of participation, more people than would otherwise be the case experience the disappointment of denial after their hopes have been raised. Evaluators should regard this as a real cost, even if it does not outweigh the benefit of determining accurately whether the ongoing allocation of resources to a program is an effective investment. That is, the indefinite expenditure of resources for an ineffective program or the failure to expand an effective one can be a substantial cost. Furthermore, as with other barriers to applying experimental methods in evaluating ongoing social programs, standard practices now mitigate the additional disappointment caused by a study. For example, researchers should train program staff how to sensitively inform control group members of their status. This training also helps gain the acceptance of program staff and reduce their discomfort in having to deny program access, another real cost. A second important practice that can reduce the frustration that control group members can feel is to be sensitive to the burden of eligibility determination (while not making changes to it that would alter the program population in important ways). It is common to provide those in the control group with a list of referrals to related services that exist in the community, as long as those services are not expected to produce a significant change in the group members' behavior or outcomes.

As suggested, overrecruitment and random assignment itself also have the potential to raise methodological concerns, specifically by altering the population served by the program or by altering the behavior of those in the control group. With respect to not changing the program population, program staff participating in an experimental evaluation should be trained not to change eligibility standards, unless this is done intentionally with well-defined criteria that can identify those who would meet the old standards and those who would not. Although it is important to monitor program eligibility criteria, not altering eligibility standards is usually feasible because most programs serve only a fraction of those who are potentially eligible. Furthermore, a central reason for evaluating social programs is to expand them if they are working well (or, of course, end or alter them if they are not). In response, knowing the effects of the program on a population larger than the current one may be more predictive of the effects of an expanded program. Finally, when it is possible to enroll a sufficiently large sample to support the appropriate subgroup analysis, a design that recruits both a sample of those who would be eligible under the program as it usually operates and an extended population is particularly powerful, because it yields unbiased estimates for both subgroups and the full treatment group (Olsen, Bell, & Luallen, 2007).

Another important issue can be where to place random assignment in the intake process of an ongoing program, because the research question that the study will address can differ depending on the point of random assignment. Placement of random assignment also has important analysis and cost implications. For example, in some of the welfare-to-work experiments, it was operationally infeasible to randomly assign recipients at the welfare office, even though they were informed there that they were required to report to an employment office or be sanctioned. Because of the infeasibility of earlier assignment, recipients were sometimes randomly assigned at the employment office, resulting in any changes in behavior caused by the initial requirement not being captured by the study. That is, estimated impacts included the effects of the services and any subsequent requirements but not the initial mandate, whereas earlier assignment would have captured both. To capture all the effects and separate out the initial mandate, sequential random assignment has been conducted when feasible, first in the welfare office and then, of those assigned to this initial treatment group, in the employment office. Those assigned to the control group at this second step received no services and were subject to no further mandates (Gueron & Rolston, 2013). More generally, although placing random assignment earlier in an intake process captures more potential effects, in some circumstances doing so can lead to treatment dilution if it results in a high no-show rate. High no-shows lead to less power and higher survey costs (no-shows still need to be surveyed even though they do not contribute information to estimates).

Although all social experiments of ongoing programs rely on a variety of the now-standard practices described previously to overcome feasibility, ethical, and substantive barriers, one design is particularly strong in mitigating all three types of barriers. Where a program is implemented in multiple locations, randomly selecting a subset of the locations to be part of the evaluation and then randomly assigning a relatively small number of individuals in each place to form a control group is highly desirable. This approach reduces or eliminates the level of required overrecruitment at any given site, mitigating feasibility, ethical, and substantive barriers. It has the added benefit of producing impact estimates that represent the program's effects on the entire target population. The Head Start Impact Study and the Job Corps Evaluation are good examples of the feasibility and value of this approach (Puma et al., 2010; Schochet, Burghardt, & McConnell, 2008).

Contexts Shift: From Individual to Place-Based Designs

In the 1980s, state and county programs that aimed at increasing the employment and earnings of welfare recipients (welfare-to-work programs) were a main venue for the increasing use of social experiments.[3] In this context, a vexing problem for evaluators was a kind of program commonly referred to as a "saturation" program that did not lend itself to individual randomized experimental designs. The program logic supporting this type of intervention was that welfare agencies needed to change the expectations of welfare recipients such that receiving benefits would be associated with making efforts to become independent through employment. To do that, some program administrators believed that it was necessary that all adults who fit certain eligibility conditions (e.g., were not disabled) be required to demonstrate that they are making an effort to become independent, thereby "saturating" the caseload and leaving no one to form a control group for an evaluation. A further program hypothesis was that changing expectations would affect not only current recipients but also those in the community who were not yet welfare recipients, causing some of those who would have applied for benefits not to do so (commonly termed "entry effects"). In response, even if a relatively small proportion of welfare applicants and recipients were exempted from participation to form a control group, an experimental evaluation based on such a design would miss the entry effects, which would occur before random assignment. More generally, a problem occurs when the intervention changes the behavior of would-be control group members, altering their outcomes such that these outcomes no longer provide a valid counterfactual (i.e., a SUTVA violation).

In certain circumstances (not the ones described here), one of these problems could be addressed in an individual-level design by conducting random assignment further upstream in the process. For example, the Income Maintenance Experiment could capture entry effects by randomly assigning individuals in the community, independent of their current welfare participation, on the assumption that widespread community knowledge of the program was not inherent in it. When such knowledge is inherent in the treatment, however, a broader solution requires identifying a control group that is outside of the community (i.e., randomizing "places" or "clusters" that were isolated from each other, some of which would operate the saturation program and some of which would not). However, substantial barriers prevented simply moving the unit of random assignment from the individual to the place.

A primary problem was misunderstanding of the implications of cluster randomized designs. A common dictum was, "Analyze at the level you

---

[3] Much of the following discussion is based on the author's experience. Although it is likely that others involved in social experiments were more knowledgeable than he and his colleagues, from talking to others he is confident such greater knowledge was not widespread in the community that practiced social experiments.

randomize." To analyze at the unit of randomization level, many more places would be necessary to obtain adequate power than could conceivably be recruited and randomized. That, however, did not prevent the occasional undertaking of place-based designs, usually with too few clusters, and subsequent violation of the dictum by analyzing data at the individual level. Some researchers would acknowledge this violation and "handle" it by saying that the design was not really an experiment but rather a quasi-experiment. Of course, this just ignored the problem rather than solving it.

The solution already existed, but in a different context, that of health research. Even in that context, it was common to simply randomize places and then analyze individuals without any further ado. But by the 1970s, health experiments existed that properly took into account that analysis done at the individual level was either too conservative (simply using the number of places assigned) or too liberal (simply using the number of individuals involved) (Donner & Klar, 2000). By 1978, researchers understood that methods parallel to those the Census used in analyzing multilevel samples were appropriate for cluster design experiments (Cornfield, 1978). This knowledge began to be applied to social experiments only in the mid-1990s and became commonplace later still, in the 2000s.

In addition to providing designs that capture social interactions that are part of an intervention, cluster designs eliminate many of the impediments of individual-level experiments, such as convincing stakeholders that random assignment of individuals is necessary and fair and training staff in how to deal with disappointed controls. In addition, the psychic costs of being denied access to a program are typically eliminated, as individuals in control clusters are seldom aware that their community does not have access to a program that operates in another community. This, of course, does not eliminate ethical issues that are raised by differential community access. Cluster designs also have feasibility and ethical impediments of their own. An experimental evaluation using a cluster design could not be applied to an existing program if it meant eliminating the program in the sites assigned to the control group. Instead, cluster designs are well suited for evaluating the effects of enhancements to existing programs or expansions to new sites, just as individual-level designs can be, depending on the nature of the enhancement or expansion.

A main feasibility problem with cluster designs is a result of their relative inefficiency: achieving the same level of power almost always requires more individuals than an individual-level design. This inefficiency arises because the individuals within each cluster typically are more similar with respect to an outcome of interest than if they were randomly assigned to the cluster. That is, some proportion of the total variance of the outcome is between clusters and not simply within them. As a result, increasing the sample within clusters beyond a relatively small number of individuals achieves little power gain, and typically, a relatively large number of clusters is required for adequate power (although far, far less than the number of individuals). The number of clusters required depends on many particular circumstances, but rarely would fewer than 30 suffice and more would be common (Schochet, 2008). This statistical inefficiency also can entail cost inefficiency. Although costs for random assignment (including both assignment and monitoring compliance with it) are almost always higher for individual than for cluster random assignment, including more individuals and more sites as is required for cluster studies almost always costs more than for a comparable study using individual assignment.

Evaluation practice has developed several approaches for reducing or mitigating the inefficiencies of cluster design. One approach is to group clusters into similar blocks before random assignment within the blocks. Another is to use cluster-level baseline characteristics as covariates to account for some of the cross-cluster variance in the analysis. The latter can have a particularly large effect in cases where a covariate is a pretest of the outcome of interest, as these are typically highly correlated. Another approach to mitigating the inefficiency of cluster designs is relying on administrative data rather than surveys since surveys are always a major cost of any evaluation. (This, of course, is also true with individual random assignment designs.)

These practices along with the inability to adequately isolate experimental and control groups, the primary motivation for conducting a place-based experiment, suggest why K–12 education has been a primary area of social policy and practice for cluster experiments. Because students group into classes and schools, individual student random assignment to, for example, a teaching practice would seldom work. However, a large school district has many schools (and even more classes) that can be randomly assigned. Because of the interest in improving standardized test outcomes, the practices described in the previous paragraphs can often be reliable: Estimate effects using administrative data and pretests as cluster-level covariates to increase power.

As mentioned previously, some of the ethical and practical issues of random assignment are the same for both cluster and individual designs. For example, the fact that some individuals have access to a program and others do not may be more visible in an individual-level design, but it is not essentially different in a cluster design. As a result, it may be hard to recruit sites when the result will be that they will operate a program, or a variant of a program, based on the toss of a coin, especially when one program is perceived to be preferable to the other. In such situations, similar to the case made to program operators with respect to individual random assignment, evaluators will need to point out the lack of strong evidence that one approach actually produces better outcomes, as well as the value of obtaining that evidence. An additional inducement that has been used with some frequency in education settings is to provide the "better" treatment to later cohorts in the control schools. For example, if the experiment is to evaluate a third-grade reading intervention, then the intervention could be provided to the next year's third-grade classes in the control schools. This assumes that this later cohort's reading outcomes will not affect the older students who were not exposed to the tested intervention, as this would preclude estimating longer term effects. And this assumption may not be reasonable with some interventions. In addition, researchers could make provision of the preferred intervention to the later cohort contingent on favorable effects on the earlier cohort.

As in the earlier illustration of the transition from using random assignment in evaluations of demonstration studies to evaluations of existing programs, the example of the application of cluster random assignment to evaluations of social programs is not intended to present new or startling information. Rather its purpose in this chapter is to suggest how many barriers to using experimental methods are best seen not as fixed and universal but as flexible and context-related. Each evaluation presents its own specific challenges that need to be addressed based on the particular research questions and circumstances at hand. By so doing, social experimenters have created a rich and evolving set of practices that have overcome many barriers to implementing randomized evaluation designs.

Current and Future Evolution: Overcoming Further Barriers

This chapter has focused on two major examples where evolving practice enabled the extension of social experiments to circumstances that otherwise would have made them infeasible, impractical, or unethical. However, many other widely held views about social experiments' inherent barriers limit the successful production of reliable evidence for policymakers and practitioners. Some of these views include the following:

- They are too costly.
- They are too often applied to programs that are not able to show effects.
- They sacrifice external validity for internal validity.
- The findings are of little practical value because at most we learn that the "black box" that is the intervention is effective or not, but nothing about why.

Each of these statements contains an element of truth. For example, many social experiments are costly, but that has little to do with random assignment itself (almost nothing to do with it in cluster designs) and primarily is a function of whether new survey-based data collection is necessary. Where main outcomes of interest reside in extent administrative data, experiments will be less costly. Moreover, the cost of an evaluation—regardless of the design—is undeniably less in the long run than the cost of letting an ineffective program or policy remain in place indefinitely or failing to expand a successful one.

Space limitations preclude an examination of each of the issues identified in this chapter. Fortunately, however, other chapters in this volume provide evidence of how practice has evolved and is evolving to address the limitations they suggest. Chapter 2 describes practices that would focus randomized trials on more promising programs. Chapters 3 and 4 address issues of external validity and how the findings of social experiments can be more generalizable. Finally, Chapters 5 through 7 address various practices that can help researchers peer into the black box and better explain the "why" of effects, or of the lack of them. Work is in progress to further expand the boundaries of social experiments.

Most policy and program debates center on claims that implementing a given program or policy will have favorable, unfavorable, or no consequences. It represents a great advance when we can move these debates beyond merely competing claims and produce reliable evidence on which claims are true and which are not. It is an even greater advance when the method that delivers this evidence is transparent, so that those whose claims are falsified cannot simply blame the messenger. In social science, randomized evaluation is our most powerful tool for establishing cause and effect, having the properties of both reliability and transparency. As a result, if we can overcome barriers to using experimental evaluation and make it available to answer more questions, as well as deepen what we learn when we use it, then we can generate evidence that can improve policies and programs.

References

Cornfield, J. (1978). Randomization by group: A formal analysis. *American Journal of Epidemiology, 108*, 100–102.

Donner, A., & Klar, N. (2000). The historical development of cluster randomized trials. In A. Donner & N. Klar (Eds.), *Design and analysis of cluster randomization experiments*. London, UK: Arnold.

Gueron, J. M., & Rolston, H. (2013). *Fighting for reliable evidence*. New York: Russell Sage Foundation.

Kershaw, D., & Fair, J. (1976). *The New Jersey Income-Maintenance Experiment: Vol. I. Operations, surveys and administration*. New York: Academic Press.

Olsen, R., Bell, S., & Luallen, J. (2007, November). *A novel design for improving external validity in random assignment experiments*. Prepared for the annual conference of the Association for Public Policy Analysis and Management, Washington, DC.

Puma, M., Bell, S., Cook, R., Heid, C., with Shapiro, G., Broene, P., . . . Spier, E. (2010). *Head Start Impact Study: Final report*. Washington, DC: U.S. Department of Health and Human Services, Administration for Children & Families.

Rubin, D. B. (1980). Randomization analysis of experimental data: The Fisher randomization test comment. *Journal of the American Statistical Association, 75*, 591–593.

Schochet, P. Z. (2008). Statistical power for random assignment evaluations of education programs. *Journal of Educational and Behavioral Statistics, 33*, 62–87.

Schochet, P. Z., Burghardt, J., & McConnell, S. (2008). Does Job Corps work? Impact findings from the National Job Corps Study. *American Economic Review, 98,* 1864–1886.

HOWARD ROLSTON *is a principal associate at Abt Associates Inc., Social and Economic Policy Division.*

Epstein, D., & Klerman, J. A. (2016). On the "when" of social experiments: The tension between program refinement and abandonment. In L. R. Peck (Ed.), *Social experiments in practice: The what, why, when, where, and how of experimental design & analysis. New Directions for Evaluation, 152*, 33–45.

2

On the "When" of Social Experiments: The Tension Between Program Refinement and Abandonment

Diana Epstein, Jacob Alex Klerman

Abstract

Modern program evaluation theory posits a rigorous impact evaluation tollgate. Programs are developed and tested via rigorous impact evaluation (often, but not exclusively, random assignment). Programs that pass this tollgate proceed to broader rollout. Results from implementing this theory are disappointing. Few programs pass the tollgate, raising the question: What now? Refine the program or abandon it? Epstein and Klerman (2012) posit that piloting and verifying the intermediate steps of the logic model can screen out programs unlikely to pass the rigorous impact evaluation tollgate. Again, that proposal raises the question: How should we proceed when a program fails to satisfy its own logic model? Refine the program or abandon it? The chapter presents several perspectives on this question and compares them against the Social Innovation Fund's experience with one of its grantees. © 2016 Wiley Periodicals, Inc., and the American Evaluation Association.

NEW DIRECTIONS FOR EVALUATION, no. 152, Winter 2016 © 2016 Wiley Periodicals, Inc., and the American Evaluation Association. Published online in Wiley Online Library (wileyonlinelibrary.com) • DOI: 10.1002/ev.20213

33

T he modern approach to developing new programs[1] posits a rigorous impact evaluation "tollgate." Programs are developed and tested via rigorous impact evaluation (often, but not exclusively, using random assignment). Programs that pass this tollgate proceed to broader rollout.

Results from implementing this approach are disappointing. Few programs pass the tollgate, raising the question: What now? Refine the program or abandon it? Epstein and Klerman (2012) posit that piloting and verifying the intermediate steps of the logic model—what they call "a falsifiable logic model tollgate"—can screen out programs unlikely to pass the rigorous impact evaluation tollgate. Again, that proposal raises the question: How should we proceed when a program fails to satisfy its own logic model? Refine the program or abandon it?

These issues are of growing urgency with the Obama administration's "innovation funds" and the tiered evidence approach. Larger funding amounts to further develop the program are conditional on showing escalating levels of evidence of effectiveness. Those programs are now beginning their second generation, such that decisions about funding a second round at a higher level of evidence and larger funding could be based on evidence from the first round. For programs with unfavorable, null, or mixed evidence in the first round, the innovation funds face the same question: Refine the program and evaluate it again or abandon it? Foundations and other funders face similar questions as the broader social policy sector begins to focus more intently on building the evidence base for what works.

But how should this "refine or abandon" decision be made? This chapter considers that question and introduces criteria for decision making. The balance of the chapter proceeds as follows. The three sections that follow provide three perspectives, each of which leads to the refine or abandon choice: the next section considers the low pass rate of programs subjected to rigorous impact evaluation; the following considers Epstein and Klerman's (2012) falsifiable logic model proposal; and the third considers statutory tiered evidence programs. Having set up the need to consider the refine or abandon choice, the next section discusses criteria that might guide making that choice, after which those criteria are applied to an example. The chapter concludes with summary and discussion.

"Implement Only Effective Programs"

The title of this section—"Implement only effective programs"—is unexceptional. No one would want to waste public funds on ineffective programs. However, the evidence is clear that that is exactly what we do. Rossi

---

[1] Similar evaluation issues apply to existing programs, but nonevaluation considerations imply that evaluation results are less determinative about future funding. The classic example is Drug Abuse Resistance Education (DARE). Consistently null evaluation results have not terminated or cut funding (on this issue, see Besharov, 2009).

predicted that half of programs don't work (i.e., Rossi's (1987) "Iron Law"; but see Rossi, 2003). Even among programs that are rigorously evaluated, the reality appears to be considerably worse than Rossi's Iron Law would suggest. Rigorous impact evaluations—often, but not exclusively, using random assignment—consistently find that the vast majority of programs have no detectable favorable impact. Even among those programs that have a detectable favorable impact, that impact is often small and fails a basic cost–benefit test (Coalition for Evidence Based Policy, 2013; Orr, 2015).

Given this bleak reality, modern program evaluation theory inserts a rigorous impact evaluation "tollgate" between program development and broad scale rollout. Only programs that pass the rigorous impact evaluation tollgate (Anderson, 2010; Society for Prevention Research, 2004)—and often a replication (McDonald, 2009; Society for Prevention Research, 2004)—proceed to broad-scale program rollout.

Nevertheless, this high rate of failure at rigorous impact evaluation raises two questions. First, can we raise the success rate of rigorous impact evaluations? And, second, what to do with programs whose impact evaluations do not find clear evidence of impact: revise or abandon?

Falsifiable Logic Models

Building on earlier discussions of "evaluability" by Wholey (1994), Epstein and Klerman (2012) posit that a "falsifiable logic model" can raise the "pass rate" for rigorous impact evaluations. They note that when a program states its logic model, it is implicitly positing a series of intermediate steps that must occur in order for the program to succeed. Those intermediate steps include (a) securing required inputs, (b) enrolling sufficient participants, (c) having sufficiently high program completion rates, (d) implementing the program with fidelity, and (e) showing simple pre/post improvement. Furthermore, they note that these intermediate steps occur in the "treatment group" and during or shortly after the end of the program. These intermediate steps are verifiable at relatively low cost; specifically, as part of an augmented conventional process and client flow analysis, without random assignment and without tracking participants well after the end of the program.

To be useful for screening programs, two additional conditions are needed. The first condition is that the programs must be required to specify a "falsifiable logic model" as part of its application for funding. Often this will mean specifying quantitative goals for enrollment rates, completion rates, fidelity, and pre/post improvement. This seems both feasible and reasonable. Epstein and Klerman note that requiring programs to specify those quantitative goals as part of their proposal for funding has a revelation property. If a site underpromises, it will not be funded initially. If it overpromises, it will not pass the rigorous impact evaluation tollgate and will not get follow-on funding. The interaction of these counterveiling pressures will induce revelation of (relatively) realistic quantitative goals for the intermediate steps of the logic model.

Second, a falsifiable logic model must actually "screen"; that is, many programs must fail their own logic model. Epstein and Klerman (2012) show that is in fact the case. For each of the five classes of intermediate outcomes, they provide multiple examples of failure to satisfy (what they infer would plausibly have been) the program's own falsifiable—usually quantitative—logic model.

Together these two points suggest that inserting a falsifiable logic model tollgate before the random assignment tollgate will screen out programs that would fail rigorous impact evaluation. As a result, the success rate for rigorous impact evaluations will rise. This is true for two reasons. First, programs that fail their own falsifiable logic model and are therefore unlikely to pass the rigorous impact evaluation tollgate will not be subject to rigorous impact evaluation. Second, some programs that fail their own falsifiable logic model can be revised and on a second (or later) try pass their own falsifiable logic model and then the rigorous impact evaluation tollgate, again raising the success rate.

Note that failure at the falsifiable logic model tollgate raises a similar issue to the one raised by failure at the rigorous impact evaluation tollgate: refine or abandon?

From Theoretical Approach to Statute

Recent trends in federal funding for programs and for program development further urge consideration of these issues. The Obama administration has launched innovation funds whose primary goal is to develop and establish the effectiveness of new program models (e.g., the U.S. Department of Education's Investing in Innovation (i3), the Corporation for National and Community Service's Social Innovation Fund (SIF); see Haskins & Margolis, 2014). Although details vary across these programs, they each adopt a tiered evidence approach. The i3 program, for example, has multiple levels of grants where larger grants (validation and scale-up) require applicants to come in with stronger evidence of impact. Then, at each level, a grantee is expected to conduct an evaluation to provide additional—and usually higher level—evidence.

The implicit vision of that additional evidence appears to be to allow grantees to move up the tiers toward clear evidence of effectiveness in order to build their evidence base and eventually secure funding from another source. Many programs begin tiered evidence funding having shown some (low) level of evidence. As part of that initial grant, the program would develop a higher level of evidence. That higher level of evidence would in turn justify a larger grant to establish an even higher level of evidence as the program scales up or expands to multiple sites.

New Directions for Evaluation • DOI: 10.1002/ev

It is still very early, but the limited (often anecdotal) evidence is consistent with the characterization of evaluation results in the introduction to this chapter. The evaluation of some programs shows clear evidence of effectiveness (at the level of evidence to be developed given the type of grant received). However, most programs will likely show null or mixed evidence of impact (again, at the level of evidence to be developed given the type of grant received). It follows that the theoretical conceptualization of an approach to program development and the implied choice—refine or abandon—will increasingly be an operational issue for federal innovation programs.

Foundations increasingly face similar issues. Foundations have traditionally been long-term funders of programs. Increasingly, they are demanding that those programs be subject to rigorous impact evaluation and that they show evidence of impact. Foundation-funded programs are likely to be like other government-funded programs in that most rigorous impact evaluations will yield mixed or null results. Then what? Should the foundation fund refining the program model that it has long funded or should the foundation abandon the program model, instead funding some new program?

The evidence suggests that, after their first rigorous impact evaluation, most programs do not show clear evidence of impact. This suggests that the "refine/abandon" choice should lean toward "abandon." However, two considerations suggest learning the other way, toward "refine." First, in some cases there do not appear to be that many other program models to substitute for those we abandon. Second, in many cases, programs also do not have to agree to be evaluated in order to be funded—they could instead seek funding from another source that does not require evaluation. As a result, if evaluation is likely to have an unfavorable outcome (i.e., program termination), then programs will not agree to be evaluated. Which way to lean will depend on the relative strength of these considerations.

Choosing Between "Refine" and "Abandon"

The previous three sections have argued that "refine or abandon?" is a crucial decision across a range of approaches to program development: a rigorous impact evaluation tollgate, a falsifiable logic model tollgate, funding at a higher level of tiered evidence, and continued foundation funding. With that framing, this section turns to how to make the refine or abandon decision. We suggest that attention should be paid to the following criteria: (a) other programs available for funding, (b) results of the initial evaluation, (c) likelihood that program changes will plausibly address failures in implementation and/or will address failures of the intervention itself, (d) goals of the evaluation and contextual factors, and (e) costs and benefits.

Other programs available for funding: First, note that there is a decision to be made by a funder, whether it be federal, state, philanthropic, or private. There are usually many more applications for funding than can be funded.

Funds going to a (or another) round of program refinement and evaluation are funds that are not available for funding evaluation of a new program.

How many more attractive program models are available for funding will be a crucial consideration. The fewer (potential) applicants for funding and the weaker are the program models in that pool, the more attractive will be program refinement. Conversely, the larger and the more promising the pool of applicants for funding, the more attractive will be terminating funding of a program that has failed some tollgate (satisfaction of the program's own falsifiable logic model or rigorous impact evaluation) and beginning funding of some new program that has not yet reached any tollgate.

Second, note that there is sometimes a built-in preference for another round of refinement. Funder staff sometimes develop an attachment to already funded programs. Existing programs are in part a reflection on funder staff; they may have had a role in selecting the programs, and they certainly had a role in nurturing and guiding the programs. Failure to fund is sometimes seen as an admission of failure. Furthermore, funder staff develop personal relationships with program staff, which can sometimes make cutting off funding hard.

Finally, it is often true that in order for programs to voluntarily undergo rigorous impact evaluation, the programs must view impact evaluation as a tool for program improvement. If the most likely outcome is mixed or null estimates of impact and those estimates could lead to program termination, why undergo rigorous impact evaluation? If the funding stream requiring rigorous impact evaluation was the only possible source of funds, programs might subject themselves to rigorous impact evaluation anyway. However, in most cases, there are other sources of funding. As a result, to induce programs to participate in funding streams requiring rigorous impact evaluation, funders lean toward program refinement rather than program abandonment.

Among the promising aspects of program improvement is building evaluation capacity. That capacity is useful both in program management (leading directly to program improvement) and in evaluation (leading indirectly to program improvement). This perspective is potentially promising because interactions with programs in the context of evaluations suggest that many well-intentioned programs lack the necessary staff, resources, and knowledge to do evaluation well. Consistent with this perspective, funders are beginning to invest considerable resources in evaluation capacity building, and the investments are perceived as likely to be cost-effective ways to improve program performance and foster learning cultures (for an empirical synthesis, see Labin, Duffy, Meyers, Wandersman, & Lesesne, 2012).

Results of the initial evaluation: Beyond these two observations—that there is a choice and that there is sometimes a preference for program refinement over program abandonment, the basic issue is what is the likely outcome of another round of evaluation? Decision makers should consider the results of the initial evaluation, in particular whether the findings are unfavorable, null, or mixed. Definitive unfavorable findings are perhaps the simplest case to handle because it means that people are potentially being harmed by the program as compared to the status quo. This is a clear indication that the program is not working and should therefore not continue to receive funding. In contrast, null findings could be the result of an underpowered study (inadequate sample) or other design flaws, or the program's effect sizes may simply be too small to detect and therefore not meaningful.

If a study was adequately powered, and if a process study indicates that the program was implemented with fidelity and it had null findings, it suggests that the program itself is not leading to effects worth pursuing. If instead the process study indicates that the program was not implemented with fidelity, the program itself may (or may not) be working, but this cannot be accurately assessed until implementation is improved (discussed in a later section). It may be worth evaluating the program again under conditions where better implementation can be assured. Of course, making this decision depends on the existence of a high-quality process study that tracked implementation, so it goes without saying that we would recommend such studies accompany rigorous impact evaluations. Finally, mixed results (some favorable, some unfavorable or null) generally suggest that the program has at least some redeeming qualities. Give the dearth of programs that work, mixed findings programs are likely worth pursuing further after program changes have been assured (discussed in a later section).

Likelihood that program changes will plausibly address failures: Next, consider the plausibility of the claim that any proposed program changes will address the failures of the falsifiable logic model. All impact evaluations have statistical noise. For a properly sized study, the conventional power analyses set the chance of a null finding given a specified minimum substantively important impact should be 20%. Unfortunately, many impact evaluations are underpowered, so the probably of a null finding when the true impact is substantively important is often greater than 20%. Nevertheless, redoing the earlier impact evaluation on the exact same program and hoping for better results seems like an unwise strategy.

Instead, the more likely source of improvement is one or more changes to the program model. It is the argument of Epstein and Klerman (2012) that a process analysis augmented with verifying the intermediate steps of a falsifiable logic model will often identify plausible explanations for why no impacts were (or would be) found; for example, failure to obtain needed resources, insufficient enrollment, low program completion rates, low fidelity of program application, and small to no gains on pre/posttest comparisons.

As such, a process evaluation is a potentially valuable protection against program failure.[2] Indeed, all the i3 evaluations are required to include implementation studies with a plan to measure fidelity of implementation of key components, a critical piece of a falsifiable logic model. This should allow evaluators and policymakers to distinguish between failures in fidelity of the intervention (did teachers actually change their behavior) versus fidelity of implementation (did teachers even show up).

If fidelity of implementation was the suggested culprit (Darrow, 2013; Darrow, Goodson, & Boulay, 2014), then how will program staff make the necessary changes to ensure that implementation proceeds "better" the second time around? Where in the logic model did implementation break down? If inputs could not be secured, what assurance do we have that conditions will change and allow for more adequate inputs? This situation may be easier to address than one in which the evaluation identifies underlying problems with the program's theory of change. This can be described as a failure of the intervention, in which the program's underlying theory has a flaw such that the assumptions behind converting inputs to outputs to outcomes is now questionable. These programs would benefit from revisiting their underlying theory and adjusting the logic model as needed before proceeding to any further evaluation.

Having identified which steps of the logic model failed, it falls to the program's proponents to write a new application for funds, and then to the funder to review the application. Such applications for funds for program refinement following an unsuccessful evaluation (either failure to satisfy the program's own falsifiable logical model or mixed or null findings in a rigorous impact evaluation) should be reviewed together with applications from new programs. As noted earlier in this section, the key question is: is this program refinement—along with another round of formative evaluation (i.e., observing the program in action and tweaking it)—more likely to yield a favorable impact than some new program concept? Evidence from the initial evaluation of this program concept would suggest not. The program was initially selected for funding because, in net, it seemed promising and likely to be effective. We now have evidence that it may be less effective that we thought.

It therefore falls to the program's proponents to provide two compelling arguments. First, the program needs to provide persuasive assurance that the proposed modifications to the details of the program design will address the failure of the intermediate steps of the logic model. Second, the program needs to provide a compelling argument that addressing that failure will be sufficient to yield favorable impacts. This second step—that is, a compelling argument that addressing that failure will be sufficient—is nontrivial. Satisfying all of the requirements of the falsifiable logic model is necessary,

---

[2] Orr (2015), on cost grounds, argues against in-depth process analysis before initial evaluation.

but not sufficient, for program impact. A program with an invalid theory of change could satisfy all of the intermediate steps of its falsifiable logic model and still not show clear evidence of favorable impact. Furthermore, when failure occurs early in the logic model (e.g., securing resources, enrolling participants, and implementing with fidelity), even addressing those early failures of the logic model may not lead to pre/post improvement and then impacts.

Goals of the Evaluation and Contextual Factors

The context must also be considered, which naturally surfaces discussions of internal validity and external validity. Evaluation may show that the program does not work in its desired context with its desired target population. This implies fundamental flaws in the logic model and suggests that the program needs to revisit basic inputs and conditions before evaluating again. In contrast, programs with promising results in one setting now attempting to scale up (e.g., the i3 scale-up grants) face an entirely different set of external validity challenges. Here, the evaluation's research question is not whether the theory is viable or the program can work, but rather if it can work in multiple places, or if it can work with the same population on a larger scale. If these evaluations show null or mixed results, it does not necessarily mean that the model is a failure. Perhaps instead adaptations are needed for new contexts or scaling-up presents new challenges not previously addressed. If the program had favorable results at least once and the failure lies in scale-up, then decision makers may reasonably decide that it is worth additional investment to try to improve the large-scale model rather than go back to the drawing board and start the development and evaluation cycle from the beginning with a new program model. Interim results may be helpful in illuminating where the original theory broke down, particularly if such results can be compared with final results across multiple indicators and among different subgroups.

Costs and Benefits

A program's new application for funding may include lowering quantitative goals of the falsifiable logic model. Changes of that form should receive increased scrutiny and programmatic changes should support those lower goals. The revelation principle continues to apply. Those making funding decisions should ask: Given lower quantitative goals, is the program still worth funding? And is it plausible that a program that only meets the lower quantitative goals will still have (sufficiently large) impacts?

Alternatively, the program may revise its outcomes as it reconsiders its fundamental theory of change. This could prove to be a desirable strategy if the revised program model is in fact better aligned with realities on the ground. A program that revises its model in this way has clearly learned from evaluation and is purporting to have made program improvements—this is an outcome of evaluation that we should seek to encourage.

An Example

Consider the case of an early subgrantee in the Social Innovation Fund tiered evidence initiative (where we omit details to preserve the anonymity of the subgrantee). The program targeted two primary ultimate outcomes. An experimental impact evaluation showed mixed findings: no impact on one primary ultimate outcome and a favorable, but not statistically significant, impact on the other primary outcome.

Now, consider satisfaction of the intermediate steps of the program's own logic model. The subgrantee had a mature program, with a stable set of partners providing a steady flow of clients. To get sufficient scale for impact evaluation, the subgrantee needed to expand. Doing so required recruiting new partners. Those new partners delivered moderately fewer clients than expected, leading to an underpowered impact evaluation. However, for the clients referred, attendance was above targets and the program appeared to have been implemented with fidelity. Process measures suggested an impact on one of the key intermediate activities, but not on the other key intermediate outcome.

This evaluation is an illustrative example of mixed findings: favorable but not significant findings in one domain, null findings in another. The secondary findings are promising but the small sample size limits the ability to draw firm conclusions about impact. The null findings—both the lack of statistically significant impact on the ultimate outcomes and the lack of change in one of the key intermediate outcomes—are surprising given the program's theory of change.

With the information gained from the evaluation, the subgrantee set out to build a learning agenda focused on determining the appropriate outcomes to expect from this population and refining the theory of change (in particular, how to shift the key intermediate outcomes). These activities have also led to revisions to the content of training for program staff.

After these changes are institutionalized, the refined program will arguably be well positioned to undergo another randomized experimental evaluation. This example shows both the importance of interpreting evaluation findings in context, and with nuance, and how under some circumstances a second evaluation might be appropriate once program refinement has occurred.

Discussion

This chapter has argued that three perspectives—a falsifiable logic model tollgate, a rigorous impact evaluation tollgate, and follow-on funding (in tiered evidence programs, foundation funding, or other public sources)—

New Directions for Evaluation • DOI: 10.1002/ev

each suggest the importance of the "revise or abandon" decision; that is, on receiving null or mixed evaluation results, should the program model be funded for another round of program refinement or should the program model be abandoned?

The discussion noted that there is a choice since there are other programs that could be developed and evaluated. How much of a choice—that is, how deep is the pool of potential program models to be tested, and how plausible are they, remains unclear and appears crucial. Acknowledging that caveat, the crucial question remains: when to continue with this program model rather than try a new program model? The discussion also noted that institutional factors sometimes bias the decision toward another round of funding, but some of those factors should arguably be leaned against. In contrast, the need to view evaluation as a tool for program improvement is real. If evaluation's only result is seen as an up or down decision on funding, inducing programs to undergo rigorous impact evaluation will be much harder.

The chapter suggested several perspectives to consider. First, the results could be noise. True impacts could be favorable and significant, but the sample was too small to detect them. More important than such statistical learning is true program refinement. Does the revised application provide a compelling case that the crucial problem with the earlier implementation has been identified and that the revised program model will ameliorate the problem? The discussion noted that insights into this question are unlikely to come from the results of the impact analysis on ultimate outcomes. Instead, any such insights will come from impact analysis of intermediate or process outcomes or, more likely, from an augmented process analysis that compares intermediate results for the treatment group to the goals specified in the program's prespecified falsifiable logic model. Requiring the submission of a falsifiable logic model along with the application and funding a process evaluation that compares results in the treatment group to that falsifiable logic model is good insurance against the possibility of null impact evaluation results.

Finally, note that the revelation property continues to apply. A program could satisfy the falsifiable logic model simply by lowering the quantifiable goals. However, funding decisions with respect to the revised application should be made considering the revised quantified goals. Are the goals now so low that the results are not worthwhile or that satisfaction of the intermediate goals is unlikely to lead to the ultimate outcomes of interest? Or were the revisions to goals consistent with the revised program model? That outcome should be encouraged.

Timing is also important. We propose to structure decision points along a continuum, building on the decision points laid out in the falsifiable logic model proposal. These decisions also depend on the age of the program, or at the very least the length of time in which model has been implemented in the tested context. Decisions may look different for long-standing programs that have been operating for many years and are poised to expand, versus programs competing at the development levels of tiered evidence grant competitions that may be more easily passed over for additional cycles of funding in favor of allocating scarce resources toward new and untested ideas. Somewhere in between these two types of government programs is the more traditional foundation approach, which is to fund a program for a while until either priorities shift or an evaluation shows a lack of impact; in the latter case, the foundation then has to consider whether to "pull the plug" or keep funding with mechanisms in place to ensure program improvement.

Fundamentally, these are issues about the probability of success of program refinement versus the probably of success of new programs. We have little to no evidence yet on that question. As the innovation programs mature, it should possible to explore this question empirically; that is, with sufficiently large samples of new and refined programs, we could estimate the success rate of new programs versus the success rate of refined programs. Those results will be specific to the decision rule used to make the refinement decision. However, assuming that funder staff can approximately rank the programs on likelihood of success on refinement, the results of such an analysis will be informative. If revised programs are more likely to succeed, fund refinement of more programs; if less likely to succeed, fund refinement of fewer programs.

Disclaimer

This chapter expresses the views of the authors. It does not represent the views of the Corporation for National and Community Service, the Office of Management and Budget, the United States Government, nor Abt Associates or its clients. Responsibility for all errors remains with the authors.

References

Anderson, D. (2010). Proven programs are the exception, not the rule [Web log post]. Retrieved from http://blog.givewell.org/2008/12/18/guest-post-proven-programs-are-the-exception-not-the-rule/

Besharov, D. J. (2009). Presidential address: From the Great Society to continuous improvement government: Shifting from "does it work?" to "what would make it better?" *Journal of Policy Analysis and Management, 28,* 199–220.

Coalition for Evidence-Based Policy. (2013). *Randomized controlled trials commissioned by the Institute of Education Sciences since 2002: How many found positive versus weak or no effects.* Washington, DC: Author. Retrieved from http://coalition4evidence.org/wp-content/uploads/2013/06/IES-Commissioned-RCTs-positive-vs-weak-or-null-findings-7-2013.pdf

Darrow, C. L. (2013). The effectiveness and precision of intervention fidelity measures in preschool intervention research. *Early Education & Development, 24,* 1137–1160.

Darrow, C., Goodson, B., & Boulay, B. (2014). *Systematizing the measurement and reporting of intervention delivery in education research.* Poster session presented at the Spring

Conference of the Society for Research on Educational Effectiveness, Washington, DC.

Epstein, D., & Klerman, J. A. (2012). When is a program ready for rigorous impact evaluation? *Evaluation Review, 36,* 373–399.

Haskins, R., & Margolis, G. (2014). *Show me the evidence: Obama's fight for rigor and results in social policy.* Washington, DC: Brookings Institution.

Labin, S., Duffy, J., Meyers, D. C., Wandersman, A., & Lesesne, C. A. (2012). A research synthesis of the evaluation capacity building literature. *American Journal of Evaluation, 33,* 307–338.

McDonald, S.-K. (2009). Scale-up as a framework for intervention, program, and policy evaluation research. In G. Sykes, B. Schneider, & D. N. Plank (Eds.), *Handbook of education policy research* (pp. 191–208). New York: Routledge.

Orr, L. L. (2015). 2014 Rossi Award Lecture: Beyond internal validity. *Evaluation Review, 39,* 167–178. doi: 0193841X15573659

Rossi, P. H. (1987). The iron law of evaluation and other metallic rules. *Research in Social Problems and Public Policy, 4,* 3–20.

Rossi, P. H. (2003, October). *The "Iron Law of Evaluation" reconsidered.* Remarks presented at the 2003 APPAM Research Conference, Washington, DC.

Society for Prevention Research. (2004). Standards of evidence: Criteria for efficacy, effectiveness and dissemination. Fairfax, VA: Author. Retrieved from http://www.preventionresearch.org/sofetext.php

Wholey, J. S. (1994). Assessing the feasibility and likely usefulness of evaluation. In J. S. Wholey, H. P. Hatry, & K. E. Newcomer (Eds.), *Handbook of practical program evaluation* (pp. 15–39). San Francisco: Jossey-Bass.

DIANA EPSTEIN *is a senior evidence analyst at the Office of Management and Budget. She was formerly a research and evaluation manager at the Corporation for National and Community Service.*

JACOB ALEX KLERMAN *is a principal associate and senior fellow at Abt Associates Inc., Social and Economic Policy Division.*

Bell, S. H., & Stuart, E. A. (2016). On the "where" of social experiments: The nature and extent of the generalizability problem. In L. R. Peck (Ed.), *Social experiments in practice: The what, why, when, where, and how of experimental design & analysis. New Directions for Evaluation, 152*, 47–59.

3

On the "Where" of Social Experiments: The Nature and Extent of the Generalizability Problem

Stephen H. Bell, Elizabeth A. Stuart

Abstract

Although randomized experiments are lauded for their high internal validity, they have been criticized for the limited external validity of their results. This chapter describes research strategies for investigating how much nonrepresentative site selection may limit external validity and bias impact findings. The magnitude of external validity bias is potentially much larger than what is thought of as an acceptable level of internal validity bias. The chapter argues that external validity bias should always be investigated by the best available means and addressed directly when presenting evaluation results. These observations flag the importance of making external validity a priority in evaluation planning. © 2016 Wiley Periodicals, Inc., and the American Evaluation Association.

Most social experiments seeking to measure the impact of government programs study nonrandomly selected individuals or geographic locations. This tendency to sample nonrepresentatively from the population of policy interest may skew measured effects of the studied intervention away from its true impact in the population. The potential for impact skewing has long been recognized in the program evaluation literature by those concerned about the generalizability, or "external validity," of research findings (see e.g., Cronbach, Gleser, Nanda, &

Rajaratnam, 1972; Green & Glasgow, 2006; Humphreys, Weingardt, & Harris, 2007; Julnes, 2011; Olsen, Bell, Orr, & Stuart, 2013; O'Muircheartaigh & Hedges, 2014; Tipton et al., 2014). In the statistics literature, there has also been increasing interest in and attention to methods for estimating population treatment effects (Bareinboim & Pearl, 2013; Hartman, Grieve, Ramsahai, & Sekhon, 2015; Kern, Stuart, Hill, & Green, 2016; Olsen & Orr, Chapter 4; Stuart, Cole, Bradshaw, & Leaf, 2011).

However, there has been surprisingly little formal investigation of how large external validity bias may be in typical evaluations, and little has been done to address this threat in the practice of social program impact evaluation.

This omission may be rectified by identifying ways to measure the bias produced in rigorous impact evaluations by nonrandom sample selection, and in particular by the inclusion of a nonrepresentative set of geographic sites in which the research is conducted. This chapter provides evaluators with four tools for investigating how much nonrepresentative site selection may bias impact findings. It addresses the external validity bias that may exist when trying to generalize impact estimates from a rigorous evaluation to a target population of interest.[1] Recently Olsen et al. (2013) have shown that external validity bias arises through the combination of three circumstances: (a) true impacts that vary from one site to another, (b) differing probabilities of inclusion in the study for these distinct sites, and (c) impact magnitudes that correlate with the probability of site inclusion. Formally, these conditions require three statistical parameters to be nonzero: the variance in site inclusion probabilities, the variance of impacts across sites, and the correlation between these two factors.

One might ask whether the typical practice of including a nonrandom set of sites in impact evaluations poses much threat to reliable findings, because tests for variation in impact magnitude across sites in the literature on large-scale social experiments have rarely produced statistically significant results. There are, however, some instances in which treatment effect heterogeneity by site has been demonstrated conclusively (e.g., see Greenberg, Meyer, Michalopoulos, & Wiseman, 2003; Hamilton, Brock, & Farkas, 1995; Nisar, 2010). Also, even where statistical tests cannot confirm that observed variation in measured impact across sites must be caused by something more than sampling variability, impact heterogeneity may exist but not be detectable from available sample sizes, which tend to be small for individual sites.[2] In light of these circumstances, we believe evaluators

---

[1] In reality, there may be multiple target populations of interest. This discussion assumes that one population of interest has been determined, but the analyses described could be repeated for multiple target populations.
[2] Limited sample sizes especially delimit the potential for statistically significant findings when conducting "difference in differences" tests using statistics with four additive

need to better understand and examine how much external validity bias may exist when trying to make policy decisions on the basis of rigorous impact evaluations. In fact, some initial research on the size of external validity bias indicates that the bias may be as large as the amount of internal validity bias that researchers tend to worry about (e.g., bias equal to 0.10 of a standard deviation of the evaluation's outcome of interest; see Bell, Olsen, Orr, & Stuart, 2016).

In this chapter, we outline four strategies for judging the presence of and magnitude of external validity bias in particular social experiments: (a) comparing sites' baseline characteristics and/or outcomes to those in the target population, (b) comparing impact findings at risk of external validity bias to impacts measured in the corresponding population, (c) directly estimating the Olsen et al. (2013) bias parameters noted previously, and (d) simulating bias under different posited site inclusion mechanisms. To illustrate the first two approaches, we present examples from existing research on experimental evaluations in the elementary education field—from a schoolwide behavior improvement intervention (Stuart, Bradshaw, & Leaf, 2015) and the national Reading First program (Bell et al., 2016). Efforts currently underway (by the authors and their collaborators) using the latter two strategies are also discussed. Future application of all four of these strategies should expand the empirical knowledge base on the extent of external validity bias in experimental evaluations, generally.

We organize our presentation into five parts. The first four sections describe and illustrate each of four strategies for moving the literature from theoretical constructs to empirical assessment of the existence and degree of the external validity bias problem in actual rigorous impact evaluations of social programs. These strategies, described in the previous paragraph, include background and outcome comparisons, impact finding comparisons, bias parameter estimation, and bias simulations. We then conclude with a discussion of next steps for research and implications for evaluation practice.

Background and Outcome Comparisons

An obvious question arises when evaluating program impacts using data from a nonrandom sample of locations: Do the selected sites "look like" the population the evaluation seeks to investigate? Existing scholarship considers two approaches for understanding sample-versus-population results from rigorous impact evaluations: (a) comparisons of background characteristics and (b) comparisons of outcomes. We describe each of these

---

components in their variance formulas, such as the estimated treatment-minus-control-group difference in mean outcomes for Site A minus the treatment-minus-control-group difference in mean outcomes for Site B.

techniques here along with their common limitation, unobserved factors that compromise the comparisons.

Comparisons of Background Characteristics

This approach measures the extent to which a given set of sites mirrors the population of interest in its background characteristics—for example, regarding various measured traits of program participants and local communities. This can be done for individual characteristics one at a time or for a summary measure, such as the probability of participation in the evaluation, expressed as a weighted average of a vector of such characteristics (Stuart et al., 2011; Tipton, 2013). The closer the study sample aligns with the population on such an indicator, the greater one's confidence that the sampled sites well represent the population. Tipton (2014) and Stuart et al. (2011) give guidelines for how close is "close enough" in this regard for reliable generalization from sample to population. A benefit of this approach is that it can be implemented using only covariate data from the sampled sites and the target population; no outcome data are required.

Comparisons of Outcomes

In addition to comparing background covariates, sometimes a comparison of outcomes can yield insights regarding the potential generalizability of study results. There are two ways this comparison can be implemented; both rely on the idea that, if two groups are similar, their average outcomes under the same treatment condition should be similar. When new interventions are evaluated, one can compare a key outcome measure or measures for "untreated" control group members from the study sites with the same outcome measure or measures—also untreated by the test intervention—taken from data on the full population of sites. The intuition here is that, if the sites in the evaluation do represent the population, their average outcomes absent the treatment should be similar to average outcomes absent the treatment in the population. This is labeled a "placebo test" by Hartman et al. (2015).

Other impact evaluations examine social programs that already treat the entire population of interest but do so experimentally by randomly excluding cases from the intervention to create control groups for measuring impact in some nonrandom subset of locations. Here, one can compare a key outcome or outcomes for cases receiving the intervention in the study sites (from the experiment's "treatment group") with the same outcome measure or measures—also treated by the intervention—taken from data on the full population of sites. The intuition here is that, if the sites in the evaluation do represent the population, their average outcomes with the treatment should be similar to average outcomes with the treatment for the population.

NEW DIRECTIONS FOR EVALUATION • DOI: 10.1002/ev

Unobserved Factors

Background comparisons and outcome comparisons share a similar limitation when used as just described to gauge external validity bias. They cannot tell researchers whether study sites differ from the population on factors (a) absent from the background characteristics and/or outcome measures examined that (b) affect the magnitude of intervention impacts. What might these factors be? Many of the unmeasured determinants of site inclusion may be idiosyncratic to particular evaluations and only evaluable through researchers' knowledge of how a given study came to include a particular set of sites. The usefulness of the comparison approaches just described depends in part on whether researchers understand from their own involvement in study set-up the ways in which included sites differ from the population.

Other determinants of site inclusion may not be idiosyncratic but exert similar influences across many evaluations. Sometimes these factors are measured and sometimes they are not. If such site inclusion factors can be identified from theory, then the research team for a given study could judge whether the background characteristics and outcome measures it is able to compare, population versus sample, encompass those (or at least the great preponderance of those) influences. Unfortunately, relatively little is known at present about the factors that influence site participation in rigorous impact evaluations and simultaneously moderate treatment effect magnitude. Stuart et al. (2016) suggest that future work "further investigate whether program effects vary [by site] (and across which factors, both individual and contextual) and account for those factors when assessing external validity" (p. 483). Some work already exists or is currently underway among evaluation researchers to quantify cross-site variation in impact magnitude and the factors that associate with impacts using data from rigorous, randomized multisite impact evaluations. Examples include Bloom, Hill, and Riccio (2005) on welfare-to-work programs and Institute of Human Development and Social Change (2015) concerning the effects of the Head Start program.

If a consistent set of correlates of impact magnitude emerge from these and related studies, future evaluations can benefit from collecting the same measures (in their particular program contexts) for all sites in the population of interest to use for diagnosing the potential for external validity bias among the subset of sites actually included in the evaluation. The "unobserved factors" problem in background characteristic checks of population and sample similarities would be ameliorated as a result.

Impact Finding Comparisons

The remaining three strategies for assessing the external validity of rigorous impact evaluations only indirectly address the reliability of the investigator's own particular evaluation. They focus instead on examining whether other

New Directions for Evaluation • DOI: 10.1002/ev

experiments—or hypothetical simulated experiments—produce or would produce externally valid impact estimates for a population of interest and, if not, by how far do they fail.

The first of these strategies extends the notion of doing *outcome* comparisons between the population and study sites (see previous discussion) to the idea of doing *impact* comparisons between the population and the study sites. It does so by paralleling the "design replication" (also known as the "within-study comparison") strand of the evaluation literature, in which researchers gauge the *internal* validity of quasiexperimental impact evaluations by comparing the impact estimates they produce to internally valid experimental estimates for the same sites (e.g., Bifulco, 2012; Cook, Shadish, & Wong, 2008; Fraker & Maynard, 1987; LaLonde, 1986). In the external validity context, the parallel design replication strategy gauges bias by comparing impact estimates between sample and population, in the special case where both estimates exist with adequate internal validity. In such circumstances, one does not *need* the sample-based finding to determine the effect of the studied intervention: the population finding of impact does so in a superior and acceptable fashion. One can use what is learned from such a comparison to determine if external validity bias is likely to be a threat in other, similarly constructed experiments for which population impact estimates are not obtainable—just as is true of the now widespread practice of deciding whether a given nonexperimental impact evaluation is adequately protected from internal validity bias by looking at the performance of its analysis approach in other studies where experimental impact measure with high internal validity can be used as a benchmark (e.g., Cook et al., 2008; Steiner, Cook, Shadish, & Clark, 2010).

In the one known application of this strategy of direct measurement of external validity bias against a rigorous benchmark, Bell et al. (2016) compare impact estimates for a population of policy interest to impact estimates from various evaluation samples to see how well or poorly the sites that real-world impact evaluation samples have actually included represent the population in terms of the ultimate goal of the research, getting the impact measure right. Bell et al. (2016) examine a setting in which rigorous estimates of the impact of an elementary school reading intervention can be constructed for all public schools in nine states. Importantly, the analysis uses lists of the school districts from those states that are actually included in 11 rigorous (mostly randomized) impact evaluations recently conducted by the U.S. Department of Education (DOE) as their hypothetical study samples. Combining "population" data from the nine states with subsets defined by the 11 sets of districts included in actual evaluations yields 11 sample-versus-population checks of external validity bias based on estimated intervention impacts. These checks are reflective of the ways 11 different rigorous DOE evaluations obtained participating sites—whether by convenience or local willingness to conduct random assignment or some other means.

NEW DIRECTIONS FOR EVALUATION • DOI: 10.1002/ev

The findings in Bell et al. (2016) indicate that the kind of school districts typically included in large-scale education evaluations have *smaller* impacts than the average impact for the entire population of interest. The average absolute "error" in the sample-based estimates equals 0.10 of the standard deviation of the outcome of interest (student reading test score) in the population—a degree of external validity bias the authors argue is large relative to several reasonable metrics for judging research reliability taken from the literature on nonexperimental study designs. The evidence to date from this innovative approach to estimating the size of external validity bias calls into question the policy relevance of impact evaluations not based on a statistically representative set of sites, at least in the field of education.

One challenge in using this approach to estimating external validity bias—which we call "population replication" analysis to parallel its "design replication" antecedent from the internal validity literature—is finding appropriate data. Rigorous impact evaluations protected from internal validity bias—that is, those based on random assignment of individual cases within sites—rarely have data for the entire population of interest, or even for a statistically representative probability sample of the population (Olsen & Orr, Chapter 4, provides strategies for getting closer to this goal). The National Job Corps Evaluation (Burghardt et al., 1999) is one exception that included the entire population of interest in an experiment, whereas the National Head Start Impact Study (Puma, Bell, Cook, & Heid, 2010) is another exception that enrolled a random sample of Head Start sites in a randomized experiment. These studies should be seen as top candidates for further direct measurement of external validity bias in nonrepresentative sites.

However, even in these studies, another challenge to estimating the size of external validity bias exists: programs evaluated by populationwide experiments such as Job Corps provide population estimates of effectiveness but do not tell us what sites *would have* participated had a less comprehensive method of site recruitment been used—an approach that yields a typical set of nonrepresentative sites. As a result, there is no realistic sample of nonrepresentative sites from which to derive (potentially biased) impact estimates under more conventional site inclusion circumstances, for comparison to the available population (or population-representative) impact.

At root, the problem is that any particular impact study will have *either* population-representative impact data *or* a nonrepresentative sample of sites, but not both. Here, it is instructive to consider how Bell et al. (2016) overcame this problem by combining three ingredients. The first was extensive data on a large set of localities that constituted a plausible population of policy interest, data that included a rich set of background variables, longitudinal outcome information, and indicators of when different sites in the database implemented the intervention of interest (Reading First). The second ingredient was lists of sites that actually participated in other randomized evaluations of educational interventions, with which to simulate different nonrepresentative evaluations of the focal intervention (Reading

First). Bell et al. (2016) were able to test whether the sites assembled for these other evaluations would have performed well in measuring the effects of Reading First. Third, the recipe required a highly refined, but admittedly not infallible, method for estimating impacts without random assignment (comparative interrupted time-series) because random assignment had not been applied to the population data set. These three ingredients can perhaps be combined in other settings to obtain further empirical estimates of the size of external validity bias in rigorous impact evaluations.

Estimation of Bias Parameters

As noted earlier, Olsen et al. (2013) have shown that external validity bias arises in multisite impact evaluations if three conditions hold simultaneously: (a) true impact magnitude varies by site, (b) the probability of study inclusion varies by site, and (c) the impact magnitude correlates with the probability of site inclusion. This formalization creates the opportunity to assess external validity bias by empirically estimating these three parameters for a particular program and evaluation context, then combining them using the formula in Olsen et al. (2013) to calculate the magnitude of external validity bias. If a technique for parameter estimation of this sort can be found, such estimation can be repeated across many evaluation and program contexts where impact evaluation involves a nonrepresentative set of sites.

With respect to the first of the three parameters, the variance of impact magnitude across sites is currently being derived by evaluators in a range of social programs contexts, as referenced earlier. Probabilities of site inclusion for actual experimental evaluations that do not select sites on a probability or populationwide basis can also be estimated regularly, at least to the extent that nonrepresentative sample are drawn based on *measured* background characteristics (see Stuart, Bell, Ebnesajjad, Olsen, & Orr, 2016, as one example). However, the third parameter—the population correlation between these two factors across sites—may not be as easy to obtain, at least not in a statistically precise way and for the right population. Unlike the estimation of the variability in site-specific impacts or in the site-specific probabilities of inclusion in experimental evaluations, the estimation of this correlation requires researchers to assemble data for individual sites showing both a numerical measure of impact magnitude and the numerical probability of inclusion in a nonrepresentative impact evaluation.

The second of these quantities is neither known nor knowable in a strict sense: all we know about an individual site is that it either was or was not included in a given evaluation. However, researchers can model the probability of participating in an evaluation by fitting models of participation as a function of observed background characteristics of program participants and community settings, which can at least give an estimate of the probability of participation. With this and site-specific impacts available on the same set of sites, the correlation between these measures can easily be calculated, as done by Allcott and Mullainathan (2012).

Unfortunately, the parameter needed in the Olsen et al. (2013) bias formula is the *population* correlation between impact and the probability of inclusion, not the *sample* correlation in a data set from a nonrepresentative experiment. From where can one obtain site-specific impact estimates for all sites in the population—and in particular, the sites *not* included in the current randomized impact evaluation? To obtain this information, it may be necessary to again return to a data set in which low-internal-validity-bias impacts can be calculated using rigorous nonexperimental methods, for individual sites across an entire population of sites. Having done so, one should consider whether calculating the Olsen et al. (2013) bias parameters adds value to the exercise—or if instead the more direct approach of measuring external validity bias in Bell et al. (2016) fully capitalizes on situations in which impacts for *all sites* in a population can be calculated. Future work should also consider how sampling error in the estimation of the three bias parameters magnifies statistical uncertainty in the resulting bias estimate once a multiplicative product of the three parameters is formed. We also encourage further thought as to whether other types of data sets or estimation strategies might be brought to bear on the challenge of quantifying the three key parameters of the Olsen et al. (2013) external validity bias formula.

Bias Simulations

A final strategy for estimating external validity bias involves simulation of the impact findings that would arise in hypothetical evaluations from different simulated nonrepresentative site selection processes. Starting from a large set of sites in which randomization of individuals to treatment or control groups provides internally unbiased impact estimates, researchers could "play" with the site-specific impact estimates pretending that various hypothetical evaluations had been conducted in which some of the available sites are included and others left out. Kern et al. (2016) use this strategy to examine how well statistical methods estimate population treatment effects under a range of different sample selection mechanisms.

Such simulations might seem to have the potential for greatly advancing our knowledge of the consequences of nonrepresentative site selection, because so many various site inclusion scenarios could be run from so many various multisite randomized evaluation data sets. One must ask, though, how convincing exercises of this sort can be made to be in two respects: how well will they mimic site inclusion mechanisms that actually arise in real world experiments? and how meaningful will be the simulation results regarding generalizability to whole populations when those results themselves derive from a nonrepresentative set of sites? This exercise would become more convincing if the collection of "building block" sites for

New Directions for Evaluation • DOI: 10.1002/ev

simulating different hypothetical estimates encompassed a meaningful population in its own right, such as in the elementary reading intervention example described previously or the Job Corps or Head Start Impact Study studies also referenced earlier. In these situations, simulated scenarios of site selection could reach across the full diversity of sites potentially included in future evaluations. The exercise would also become more convincing if site selection for the simulations were guided by actual patterns of site inclusion in real-world evaluations—a goal that can be pursued using approaches described earlier for modeling the types of sites that tend to participate in rigorous impact evaluations.

Future Research and Implications for Practice

This chapter presents initial thinking on how to gauge the extent of external validity bias in rigorous evaluations of social programs. Until recently, almost no formal attention has been given to potential *external* validity bias in studies whose susceptibility to internal validity bias has been alleviated by using random assignment. Almost nothing is known about the size of external validity bias in the large portfolio of completed experimental impact studies nor about how that bias may affect the usefulness of findings from those evaluations as guides to policy decisions. In fact, almost no attention has been given to understanding the processes through which some sites participate in rigorous evaluations and others do not. We believe that better documentation of these processes, and the resulting samples that emerge, is a crucial first step in understanding how much we need to be concerned about external validity bias. This may include quantitative work such as that described here, as well as qualitative studies to better understand how researchers select sites to participate and how sites decide whether or not to do so.

The premise of all of the methods examined in this chapter is that policymakers have a population in mind when seeking to anticipate the effectiveness of social programs, a population to which they would like to apply results from a rigorous evaluation. We urge policymakers also to ask another question beyond "What impact is measured in an available evaluation?" Of equal importance is the question "Does the available evaluation provide findings close to correct for the population of policy interest?" A key component of nearly all the strategies discussed here for answering the latter question is the combining of information on both the population of interest and on the sites actually included in particular evaluations. Although some insight can be gained by simply comparing background characteristics between the sample and the target population, having outcome data—or, even better, estimated impacts—for the population can provide major additional progress.

We highlight the need for high-quality, expansive data on populations of policy interest to facilitate the use of the methods described here. We

also encourage researchers to consider novel ways of combining population data and data from rigorous evaluations to estimate the size of external
validity bias. We hope that a broader research base on this topic—a "population replication" literature—can be built up by these efforts, just as the
design replication literature assessing internal validity bias in nonexperimental studies has been established over the past 30 years. Obtaining information on the magnitude of the problem constitutes the first crucial step
toward ensuring that in the future, the results of rigorous impact evaluations are interpreted and used appropriately for policymaking purposes.

Acknowledgments

The research reported here was supported in part by the Institute of Education Sciences, U.S. Department of Education, through grant R305D100041
to Abt Associates Inc., and the National Science Foundation, through grant
DRL-1335843 to Johns Hopkins University.

References

Allcott, H., & Mullainathan, S. (2012). *External validity and partner selection bias* (NBER
   Working Paper No. w18373). Cambridge, MA: National Bureau of Economic Re-
   search.
Bareinboim, E., & Pearl, J. (2013). A general algorithm for deciding transportability of
   experimental results. *Journal of Causal Inference, 1*, 107–134.
Bell, S. H., Olsen, R. B., Orr, L. L., & Stuart, E. A. (2016). Estimates of external validity
   bias when impact evaluations select sites non-randomly. *Educational Evaluation and
   Policy Analysis, 38*, 318–335. doi:10.3102/0162373715617549
Bifulco, R. (2012). Can nonexperimental estimates replicate estimates based on random
   assignment in evaluations of school choice? A within-study comparison. *Journal of
   Policy Analysis and Management, 31*, 729–751.
Bloom, H. S., Hill, C. J., & Riccio, J. A. (2005). Modeling cross-site experimental differences to find out why program effectiveness varies. In H. S. Bloom (Ed.), *Learning
   more from social experiments: Evolving analytic approaches*. New York: Russell Sage
   Foundation.
Burghardt, J., McConnell, S., Meckstroth, A., Schochet, P., Johnson, T., & Homrighausen, J. (1999). *National Job Corps Study: Report on study implementation*. Princeton, NJ: Mathematica Policy Research, Inc. Retrieved from https://wdr.doleta.gov/
   opr/fulltext/99-jc_implement.pdf
Cook, T. D., Shadish, W. R., & Wong, V. C. (2008). Three conditions under which experiments and observational studies produce comparable causal estimates: New findings
   from within-study comparisons. *Journal of Policy Analysis and Management, 27*, 724–
   750.
Cronbach, L. J., Gleser, G. C., Nanda, H., & Rajaratnam, N. (1972). *The dependability of
   behavioral measurements: Theory of generalizability for scores and profiles*. New York:
   Wiley.
Fraker, T., & Maynard, R. (1987). The adequacy of comparison group designs for evaluations of employment-related programs. *Journal of Human Resources, 22*, 194–227.
Green, L. W., & Glasgow, R. E. (2006). Evaluating the relevance, generalization, and
   applicability of research: Issues in external validation and translation methodology.
   Evaluation & the Health Professions, 29, 126–153.

Greenberg, D., Meyer, R., Michalopoulos, C., & Wiseman, M. (2003). Explaining variation in the effects of welfare-to-work programs. *Evaluation Review, 27,* 359–394.

Hamilton, G., Brock, T., & Farkas, J. (1995). *The JOBS evaluation: Early lessons from seven sites.* Washington, DC: U.S. Department of Health and Human Services, Administration for Children and Families, Office of the Assistant Secretary for Planning and Evaluation.

Hartman, E., Grieve, R., Ramsahai, R., & Sekhon, J. S. (2015). From sample average treatment effect to population average treatment effect on the treated: Combining experimental with observational studies to estimate population treatment effects. *Journal of the Royal Statistical Society: Series A (Statistics in Society), 178,* 757–778.

Humphreys, K., Weingardt, K. R., & Harris, A. H. S. (2007). Influence of subject eligibility criteria on compliance with national institutes of health guidelines for inclusion of women, minorities, and children in treatment research. *Alcoholism: Clinical and Experimental Research, 31,* 988–995.

Institute of Human Development and Social Change. (2015). *Secondary analysis of variation in impacts of Head Start center.* New York: New York University. Retrieved from http://steinhardt.nyu.edu/ihdsc/savi

Julnes, G. (2011). Reframing validity in research and evaluation: A multidimensional, systematic model of valid inference. In H. T. Chen, S. I. Donaldson, & M. M. Mark (Eds.), *New Directions for Evaluation: No. 130. Advancing validity in outcome evaluation: Theory and practice* (pp. 55–67). San Francisco, CA: Jossey-Bass. doi:10.1002/ev.365

Kern, H. L., Stuart, E. A., Hill, J., & Green, D. P. (2016). Assessing methods for generalizing experimental impact estimates to target populations. *Journal of Research on Educational Effectiveness, 9,* 103–127.

LaLonde, R. J. (1986). Evaluating the econometric evaluations of training programs with experimental data. *American Economic Review, 76,* 604–620.

Nisar, H. (2010). Do charter schools improve student achievement? Unpublished manuscript, Department of Economics, University of Wisconsin, Madison. Retrieved from http://www.ssc.wisc.edu/~scholz/Seminar/Charter_School_MPS.pdf

Olsen, R. B., Bell, S. H., Orr, L. L., & Stuart, E. A. (2013). External validity in policy evaluations that choose sites purposively. *Journal of Policy Analysis and Management, 32,* 107–121.

O'Muircheartaigh, C., & Hedges, L. V. (2014). Generalizing from unrepresentative experiments: A stratified propensity score approach. *Journal of the Royal Statistical Society: Series C (Applied Statistics), 63,* 195–210.

Puma, M., Bell, S., Cook, R., & Heid, C., with Shapiro, G., Broene, P., ... Spier, E. (2010). *Head Start Impact Study: Final report.* Washington, DC: U.S. Department of Health and Human Services, Administration for Children & Families.

Steiner, P. M., Cook, T. D., Shadish, W. R., & Clark, M. H. (2010). The importance of covariate selection in controlling for selection bias in observational studies. *Psychological Methods, 15,* 250.

Stuart, E. A., Bell, S. H., Ebnesajjad, C., Olsen, R. B., & Orr, L. L. (2016). Characteristics of school districts that participate in rigorous national educational evaluations. *Journal of Research on Educational Effectiveness.*

Stuart, E. A., Bradshaw, C. P., & Leaf, P. J. (2015). Assessing the generalizability of randomized trial results to target populations. *Prevention Science, 16,* 475–485.

Stuart, E. A., Cole, S., Bradshaw, C. P., & Leaf, P. J. (2011). The use of propensity scores to assess the generalizability of results from randomized trials. *Journal of the Royal Statistical Society, Series A, 174,* 3969–3386.

Tipton, E. (2013). Improving generalizations from experiments using propensity score subclassification: Assumptions, properties, and contexts. *Journal of Educational and Behavioral Statistics, 38,* 239–266.

Tipton, E. (2014). How generalizable is your experiment? Comparing a sample and population through a generalizability index. *Journal of Educational and Behavioral Statistics, 39*, 478–501.

Tipton, E., Hedges, L., Vaden-Kiernan, M., Borman, G., Sullivan, K., & Caverly, S. (2014). Sample selection in randomized experiments: A new method using propensity score stratified sampling. *Journal of Research on Educational Effectiveness, 7*, 114–135.

STEPHEN H. BELL *is a vice president and senior fellow at Abt Associates Inc., Social and Economic Policy Division.*

ELIZABETH A. STUART *is a professor at the Bloomberg School of Public Health, The Johns Hopkins University.*

NEW DIRECTIONS FOR EVALUATION • DOI: 10.1002/ev

Olsen, R. B., & Orr, L. L. (2016). On the "where" of social experiments: Selecting more representative samples to inform policy. In L. R. Peck (Ed.), *Social experiments in practice: The what, why, when, where, and how of experimental design & analysis. New Directions for Evaluation, 152,* 61–71.

4

On the "Where" of Social Experiments: Selecting More Representative Samples to Inform Policy

Robert B. Olsen, Larry L. Orr

Abstract

Most social experiments are conducted in samples of sites that are not formally representative of the population of policy interest. These studies may produce impact estimates that are unbiased for the sample but biased for the population from which the sample was selected. Recent research has estimated the bias associated with nonrandom inclusion. Although some research has focused on solutions to the problem at the design stage or the analysis stage, research on ways to address this problem is still sparse. This paper provides four recommendations to help researchers obtain more representative samples in impact studies. The fundamental challenge is that, in most impact studies, sites are not required to participate if selected. Therefore, obtaining a sample that adequately represents the population of policy interest can be difficult, and the resulting impact estimates may suffer from external validity bias. The recommendations in this chapter address this challenge to help researchers obtain more representative samples when obtaining a perfectly representative sample is not possible. The recommendations, which are based on standard survey sampling methods, demonstrate that researchers can take practical steps to obtain impact estimates that are more generalizable from the study sample to the broader population of policy interest—and therefore more relevant for informing policy decisions. © 2016 Wiley Periodicals, Inc., and the American Evaluation Association.

NEW DIRECTIONS FOR EVALUATION, no. 152, Winter 2016 © 2016 Wiley Periodicals, Inc., and the American Evaluation Association. Published online in Wiley Online Library (wileyonlinelibrary.com) • DOI: 10.1002/ev.20207

I mpact evaluations based on prospective research designs, including randomized experiments, usually select a sample in two stages. In the first stage, the evaluators select a sample of "sites" defined by geography (e.g., counties) or local administrative units (e.g., welfare offices, school districts). In the second stage, they select units (individuals or groups of individuals, such as classrooms or families) within each site.

In most impact evaluations, the sites are not required to participate in the evaluation. If some sites refuse to participate, the sites included in the study may not be representative of the population from which they were selected and hence of the population affected by the policy decisions likely to be influenced by the study's findings. Anticipating the challenges in obtaining cooperation from sites, researchers rarely even try to recruit a representative sample of sites and instead select a convenience or purposive sample of sites from the outset that at best is designed to match the population of policy interest on a small number of observed characteristics.

Nonrandom site selection can potentially lead to biased impact estimates for the broader population(s) from which participating sites were selected. Olsen, Bell, Orr, and Stuart (2013) provide a formal model for purposive site selection, define external validity from purposive site selection as the difference between the average impact in a purposive sample and the true average impact in the population of policy interest—defined as the population that would be affected by the policy decision(s) the study is intended to inform—and derive a mathematical expression for this bias. This expression shows that this bias, which Olsen et al. refer to as "external validity bias," arises if (a) the probabilities of sites participating in the evaluation vary, (b) treatment effects vary, and (c) the correlation between those two quantities is nonzero. In other words, external validity bias becomes a problem when there is treatment effect heterogeneity and the factors that influence whether sites participate also influence the magnitude of the impact. Because the existence of these conditions cannot be known in advance (or, in most cases, after the fact), studies that select sites nonrandomly begin with the risk that the resulting impact estimates will be biased.

The only sure way for an evaluation to avoid external validity bias is for it to obtain a random sample of sites. Doing so requires sampling sites randomly and obtaining cooperation from all or a random sample of these sites. In this chapter, we focus on the former—the selection of sites. However, the concluding section reflects on the latter as well as other approaches to improving the external validity of impact evaluations.

Recent empirical research has attempted to quantify the magnitude of the external validity bias from purposive site selection. Bell, Olsen, Orr, and Stuart (2016) estimate the bias from conducting a hypothetical evaluation of the Reading First education program in a purposive sample to be approximately 0.10 standard deviations: This is twice the (admittedly arbitrary) threshold set by the What Works Clearinghouse for acceptable levels of attrition bias in randomized experiments (What Works Clearinghouse, 2014). It is also twice as large as the bias from using a differences-in-differences model, whose internal validity many researchers would question. Furthermore, Allcott (2015) and Allcott & Mullainathan, 2012 find evidence of external validity bias, which they call "partner selection bias," in evaluations of the impact of energy conservation programs.

Very little research considers solutions to the problems that arise from nonrandom site selection into experimental evaluations. Recent work (Tipton, 2013a; Tipton & Peck, 2016) has proposed a design-based approach that ensures that the nonrandom sample of participating sites successfully recruited for an experiment matches the population of interest on a set of observed characteristics. However, this approach may still produce impact estimates with external validity bias if unobserved site-level characteristics influence both site-level decisions about participating and the impact of the intervention in their sites. Other research has focused on analysis-based solutions once an unrepresentative set of sites is obtained; these solutions involve post-hoc statistical corrections for differences between the sample and the population on characteristics observed for both the sample and the population (e.g., Cole & Stuart, 2010; Kern, Stuart, Hill, & Green, 2016; Stuart, Cole, Bradshaw, & Leaf, 2011). Bell and Stuart (Chapter 3) discuss such approaches. Here, we focus on design-based methods.

Contribution of the Chapter

In this chapter, we make four recommendations for how to obtain more representative samples for impact evaluations. These recommendations are designed to obtain samples that are similar to the population of interest on both observed and unobserved characteristics. Obtaining a sample that is similar to the population on unobserved characteristics, as well as observed characteristics, is important in settings where the combination of theory and empirical evidence leaves uncertainty about the factors driving impact variation across sites. In this context, many of the site-level factors influencing site-level impacts are likely to be unobserved (because no one thought to collect data on those factors).

To obtain more representative samples in experimental impact evaluations, we recommend a strategy that relies heavily on random selection. The remainder of this chapter more fully articulates our proposed strategy, and each of the four recommendations that comprise this strategy.

Recommendation 1: Identify the Population of Policy Interest

Social experiments are conducted to inform policy decisions. Remarkably, many, if not most evaluations do not even attempt to specify the policy decision they are intended to inform or the population that would be affected by that policy decision. We view clear identification of this population (which we refer to as the "population of policy interest" and Tipton et al., 2014, refer to as the "inference population") as an essential first step in sample selection. As we will see, this is not always straightforward, a fact that may explain why many evaluators simply skip this step. Failure to identify the population of interest, however, especially when coupled with nonrandom sample selection, leaves the user of evaluation results with almost no guidance as to the applicability of the results beyond the evaluation sample itself.

To identify the population of policy interest, evaluators may wish to ask themselves the following questions:

• What policy decisions do we hope to inform with the results of our experiment?
• Whom would those policy decisions affect (i.e., which individuals, businesses, schools, states, offices)?
• Which group or groups of potentially affected individuals or entities are of greatest interest to policymakers?

One way to answer these questions is to focus on the population of interest to the evaluation sponsor that funded the study. Although other entities also may use the results to inform policy decisions that they face, the primary goal of an experiment is typically to inform a policy decision faced by the experiment's sponsor. Therefore, in this chapter, we focus on the population of interest to the study's research sponsor, given the sponsor's goals in conducting the impact evaluation.[1]

Identifying the population(s) of interest requires communication with the evaluation sponsor and careful thinking about the goal(s) of the experiment. If an evaluation is designed to inform the decision of whether to keep or eliminate an existing program, the population of interest could be current and future participants in places where the program currently operates. This is probably the population of policy interest in most evaluations of established federal programs. For example, the population of interest for the National Job Corps Study (Schochet, Burghardt, & McConnell, 2008) was probably all Job Corps participants nationwide, whereas the population of interest for the Head Start Impact Study (Puma, Bell, Cook, & Heid, 2010) was probably all Head Start participants nationwide. However, the population of interest in these studies might be defined more broadly to include all *eligible* individuals, including eligible nonparticipants, because they are the intended beneficiaries of the program.

[1] At the same time, we recognize that research funded by one sponsor may be used by a separate entity to inform policy decisions that it faces. For example, the state of California may fund an experiment to inform a state policy decision, but the state of Massachusetts may be interested in using the results to inform the same or similar policy decisions faced by state policymakers in Massachusetts.

NEW DIRECTIONS FOR EVALUATION • DOI: 10.1002/ev

If the evaluation is designed to inform the policy decision of whether to expand a program, the population of interest may include only individuals who are *not* currently participating in the program. For example, the population of interest might be eligible nonparticipants in places where the program is not currently operating who could potentially participate if the program were expanded, or eligible nonparticipants in existing program communities who might participate if program targeting were broadened, program outreach were more aggressive, or program funding were increased in existing program sites.

Evaluations are sometimes categorized into "effectiveness" and "efficacy" studies. Effectiveness studies are explicitly intended to measure the effects of the intervention on the population of interest. Efficacy studies are conducted to determine whether an intervention has a positive effect under favorable conditions, and the results are interpreted as evidence of whether an effectiveness study is warranted.

Defining the population of interest is absolutely essential in effectiveness studies. Effectiveness studies are used to determine whether some population is (or would be) better off with the program than without. However, even efficacy studies that assess whether the program or intervention has impacts under favorable conditions would benefit from having a well-defined population of interest. It would be useful for evaluators conducting efficacy trials to clarify the conditions thought to be favorable (e.g., sites that demonstrate a particular capacity believed to be important for implementing the intervention with high fidelity) and to define the population of interest to include sites in which these favorable conditions are present. Defining the population of interest would help policymakers understand the conditions under which an intervention has been shown to work (or not work); it would also help to identify conditions under which the intervention has not yet been tested, to inform future research.

Recommendation 2: Develop a Sampling Frame

Once the population of interest is defined, evaluators need a sampling frame from which to select sites. Although a sampling frame may not be necessary to identify a convenience sample of volunteers, it is essential for any type of sampling from the larger population (random or otherwise).

In many evaluations, a sampling frame of all sites in the population may be readily available. For example, in evaluations of federal grant programs, the federal agency sponsoring the evaluation will be able to provide a list of all current grantees (if the list is not publicly available online). In evaluations of educational programs, the Common Core of Data maintained by the National Center for Education Statistics at the U.S. Department of Education provides a census of public schools and school districts that can be used to construct a sampling frame when the population of interest consists of some subset of public school students. Similar sampling frames exist in other policy areas.

In other evaluations, there may be no ready-made listing of the universe of possible sites to serve as a sampling frame, and the researchers may need to construct the list themselves (e.g., see Tipton and Peck, 2016, for a discussion of this issue in the context of welfare evaluations). In such cases, the sampling frame need not include all eligible sites in the population of interest (because constructing such a frame could be prohibitively expensive). Evaluators can instead randomly select geographic areas or political jurisdictions, identify all eligible sites within those areas, and select from those sites, in a process similar to multistage probability sampling designs commonly used in survey research. This is effectively the same as, and in terms of bias risk statistically equivalent to, having the entire universe in the enumerated frame.

For example, suppose that evaluators were conducting an evaluation of home health care providers. The evaluators could select a random sample of counties—perhaps oversampling large counties—canvas the selected counties to identify all of the home health care providers located within them, and select a random sample of the service providers that were identified in these counties. The resulting sample could be weighted using the selection probability to represent the full population of home health care providers nationwide.

Recommendation 3: Select Sites Randomly

As noted earlier, the only way to be sure that the evaluation sites represent the larger population of interest is to select them randomly from that population. Selecting sites randomly will not guarantee that the resulting sample will be representative of the population if sites can opt out of the study. However, it will guarantee that within sampling error, the sites *recruited* to participate will be statistically equivalent to the population on both observed and unobserved factors. This seems to us a major advantage over starting with a sample of unknown external validity. Random selection of sites allows us to weight sites by the inverse of their selection probability, as we do in surveys, and to reweight for nonparticipation of selected sites, as we do to correct for nonresponse in surveys.

In selecting sites randomly, researchers could select a simple random sample from the sampling frame of eligible sites. Simple random sampling ensures that there are no systematic differences between the sample of selected sites and the population of sites from which they were selected.

However, in practice, stratified random sampling—that is, stratifying the sites into groups and then selecting a simple random sample from each group—has an important advantage over simple random sampling: It ensures that the composition of the sampled sites is identical to that of the population from which it was selected on each of the stratifying variables.

NEW DIRECTIONS FOR EVALUATION • DOI: 10.1002/ev

By removing chance differences on these factors between the sample and the population, stratified random sampling can improve both the face validity of the sample for estimating average impacts in the population and the statistical precision of the analysis.

To obtain more precise estimates of the average impact in the population, strata should be defined based on factors that the evaluator expects to be associated with the impacts of the intervention.[2] For example, if the effects of the intervention might be expected to vary with the size of the local program, then the sampling frame of potential sites could be stratified by size (e.g., dividing sites into large and small or large, medium, and small before selecting a random sample within the strata). Selecting stratifiers that are likely to be associated with the impacts of the intervention requires theory—or at least some hard thinking—and clearly benefits from empirical evidence. In the absence of either theory or evidence, evaluators may want to consider conducting a cluster analysis to identify a smaller number of groups that are similar on a larger number of variables (Tipton, 2013a; Tipton & Peck, 2016). Finally, the maximum number of strata is constrained by the number of sites to be selected (see Orr, 1999, for more guidance on the optimal number of sites).

The principal critique of random site selection is that if sites can opt out of the study, random site selection may be of little benefit. We acknowledge that random site selection is not sufficient to eliminate external validity bias. However, it is a *necessary* first step toward producing externally valid impact estimates unless selection into the study is ignorable conditional on observed site-level characteristics (Tipton, 2013b). This condition is unlikely to hold in the real world, where intervention effects vary along dimensions that are not captured by the data collected.

The ability to recruit randomly selected sites will depend heavily on the specific circumstances of the evaluation. In the National Job Training Partnership Act (JTPA) Study, roughly 90% of the sites approached refused to participate, largely for reasons very specific to the JTPA program (Doolittle & Traeger, 1990). The evaluation of the Food Stamp Employment and Training Program (Puma & and Burstein, 1994), on the other hand, achieved an 80% participation rate, resulting in a sample of 53 randomly selected sites, and the National Head Start Evaluation (Puma et al., 2010) included 87 of the 90 eligible grantees that were randomly selected for the study. These efforts demonstrate the feasibility of the approach in at least some circumstances. More generally, the only way to learn how broadly the approach can be applied, and under what conditions, and to develop more effective recruiting techniques, is for evaluators to try to implement random selection of sites. With this chapter, we hope to provide a roadmap for evaluators to begin to do so with greater frequency.

---

[2] Evaluators may also select stratifiers for other purposes, such as improving statistical power in making subgroup comparisons between different types of sites.

This brief discussion of site recruitment within evaluations highlights the practical obstacles that exist in the field. Because some sites will refuse to participate, researchers must choose backup sites to replace nonparticipating sites. The simplest way to do this is to replace nonparticipating sites with other randomly selected sites from the same sampling frame or stratum. If the number of refusals is high, we also recommend selecting a random subset of the refusing sites for more intensive recruitment efforts, perhaps with additional inducements to participate. The random subset of refusing sites can be "weighted up" to represent all refusing sites to produce a more representative sample with less external validity bias.

Recommendation 4: Set Sample Sizes to Account for Random Site Selection

Evaluators routinely set sample size targets for their evaluations to achieve the desired power for "fixed effects" impact analysis (i.e., analysis of the effects within the sample of participating sites). But policy interest seldom focuses on particular sites. The U.S. Department of Labor may test a new job search approach in Dayton and Kalamazoo, but it is not interested in the impacts in those two cities per se. It is interested in what the effects in those two cities reveal about what the effects might be in the rest of the country. For that purpose, the standard error of the fixed effects estimator gives a biased measure of the uncertainty attached to evaluation estimates because it omits a critical part of the variance of the estimate—the sampling error associated with choosing those two sites rather than any other two (or more) sites in the nation.

To compensate for sampling error when selecting sites randomly, larger samples are needed. As shown in Schochet (2008), the increase in sample size requirements depends entirely on the variation in impacts across sites (see equation 7 in Schochet): The larger the cross-site variation in impacts, the greater the sample required to detect impacts from a random sample of these sites. Selecting sites randomly may increase sample size requirements for one additional reason: The effects of the intervention may be smaller in a random sample of sites than it would be in a purposive sample of sites because purposive selection is often designed to select sites in which the conditions are favorable for positive impacts (as in efficacy trials).

Although larger samples certainly increase the cost of any evaluation, the main alternative and status quo—purposive site selection with smaller samples—has serious limitations that reduce the value of the evaluation findings. Purposive site selection yields evidence that cannot be confidently generalized to the populations of interest to policymakers. Fixed effects analysis, as mentioned earlier, does not properly account for the uncertainty in the estimation—and therefore understates the "risk" associated with making whatever policy decisions the evaluation was designed to inform. In contrast, random site selection is a necessary first step toward producing evidence that can be confidently generalized to the populations of interest to policymakers (those that their policy decisions would affect).

Future Directions

As we asserted earlier, random site selection is a necessary first step to obtaining a representative sample, but it is not sufficient. To be confident that the results from the sample generalize to the population of policy interest requires that the random sample of sites agrees to participate in the study. Except in those cases where sites are effectively required to participate in an evaluation—as when funding agencies include evaluation requirements in grant notifications and agreements—it is probably not realistic to expect all sites to agree to participate. Therefore, it is important to consider additional approaches to produce more externally valid and useful evidence to inform policymakers.

In our assessment, three potentially fruitful approaches may produce more externally valid impact evaluations. The first approach involves designing studies to substantially increase sites' motivation to participate. Low take-up rates are arguably the primary challenge in conducting experimental evaluations. Improvements in design or smarter incentives would be welcomed, both to increase the number of randomized experimental evaluations that are conducted and to increase the chances that the resulting samples are representative of the populations from which they were chosen. Advances in behavioral sciences have been exploited to develop low-cost interventions that yield substantial behavioral responses by individuals; behavioral science may hold the key to developing design enhancements, marketing, or financial incentives that would encourage more sites to participate in experimental impact evaluations.

The second approach involves increased use of analytic methods which were designed for other purposes but that may be useful in reducing external validity bias from unrepresentative samples. For example, a nonrandom sample can be reweighted to more closely match the population of interest on observed characteristics (e.g., see Cole & Stuart, 2010; Stuart et al., 2011). To the extent that matching reduces differences between the sample and the population that are associated with impacts, this will reduce external validity bias. Other more sophisticated methods have been developed to relax some of the restrictive assumptions of standard methods (e.g., see the use of Bayesian Additive Regression Trees in Hill, 2011 and Kern, Stuart, Hill, & Green, 2016).

The third potentially fruitful direction would be increased development and application of methods to estimate external validity bias, as discussed in Bell and Stuart (Chapter 5). For example, when the take-up rate in an experiment is low, a quasi-experimental design may be a useful complement because it could be implemented in both the sites that agreed to participate in the experiment and in sites that refused to participate but agreed to implement the intervention (if they had not already). A quasi-experimental design could involve matched comparison sites or individuals. To estimate the external validity bias generated by site refusals, researchers could compare quasi-experimental impact estimates for the sites that agreed to participate in the experiment to quasiexperimental impact estimates for the sites that refused to participate. Kaizar (2011) formalizes this approach and shows how the quasiexperimental and experimental estimates can be combined to reduce external validity bias. The results from this kind of analysis may suggest that the findings from the experiment either overstate or understate the average impacts in the broader population—potentially useful information to policymakers who have to predict the likely consequences of different policy decisions.

Acknowledgments

The research reported here was supported in part by the Institute of Education Sciences, U.S. Department of Education, through grant R305D100041 to Abt Associates Inc., and the National Science Foundation, through grant DRL-1335843 to Johns Hopkins University.

References

Allcott, H. (2015). Site selection bias in program evaluation *The Quarterly Journal of Economics*, *130*(3), 1117–1165.

Allcott, H., & Mullainathan, S. (2012). *External validity and partner selection bias* (NBER Working Paper No. w18373). Cambridge, MA: National Bureau of Economic Research.

Bell, S. H., Olsen, R., Orr, L. L., & Stuart, E. A. (2016). Estimates of external validity bias when impact evaluations select sites non-randomly. *Educational Evaluation and Policy Analysis*, *38*, 318–335. doi:10.3102/0162373715617549

Cole, S. R., & Stuart, E. A. (2010). Generalizing evidence from randomized clinical trials to target populations: The ACTG-320 trial. *American Journal of Epidemiology*, *172*, 107–115.

Doolittle, F., & Traeger, L. (1990). *Implementing the National JTPA Study*. New York: Manpower Demonstration Research Corporation.

Hill, J. L. (2011). Bayesian nonparametric modeling for causal inference. *Journal of Computational and Graphical Statistics*, *20*, 217–240. doi:10.1198/jcgs.2010.08162

Kaizar, E. E. (2011). Estimating treatment effect via simple cross design synthesis. *Statistics in Medicine*, *30*, 2986–3009.

Kern, H. L., Stuart, E. A., Hill, J., & Green, D. P. (2016). Assessing methods for generalizing experimental impact estimates to target populations. *Journal of Research on Educational Effectiveness*, *9*(1), 103–127.

Olsen, R., Bell, S. H., Orr, L., & Stuart, E. A. (2013). External validity in policy evaluations that choose sites purposively. *Journal of Policy Analysis and Management*, *32*, 107–121.

Orr, L. L. (1999). *Social experiments: Evaluating public programs with experimental methods*. Thousand Oaks, CA: Sage Publications.

Puma, M., Bell, S., Cook, R., & Heid, C., with Shapiro, G., Broene, P., ... Spier, E. (2010). *Head Start Impact Study: Final report*. Washington, DC: U.S. Department of Health and Human Services, Administration for Children & Families.

Puma, M. J., & Burstein, N. R. (1994). The National Evaluation of the Food Stamp Employment and Training Program. *Journal of Policy Analysis and Management, 13*, 311–330.

Schochet, P. Z. (2008). Statistical power for random assignment evaluations of education programs. *Journal of Educational and Behavioral Statistics, 33*, 62–87.

Schochet, P. Z., Burghardt, J., & McConnell, S. (2008). Does Job Corps work? Impact findings from the National Job Corps Study. *American Economic Review, 98*, 1864–1886.

Stuart, E. A., Cole, S., Bradshaw, C. P., & Leaf, P. J. (2011). The use of propensity scores to assess the generalizability of results from randomized trials. *Journal of the Royal Statistical Society, Series A, 174*, 3969–3386.

Tipton, E. (2013a). Stratified sampling using cluster analysis: A sample selection strategy for improved generalizations from experiments. *Evaluation Review, 37*, 109–139.

Tipton, E. (2013b). Improving generalizations from experiments using propensity score subclassification: Assumptions, properties, and contexts. *Journal of Educational and Behavioral Statistics, 38*, 239–266.

Tipton, E., Hedges, L., Vaden-Kiernan, M., Borman, G., Sullivan, K., & Caverly, S. (2014). Sample selection in randomized experiments: A new method using propensity score stratified sampling. *Journal of Research on Educational Effectiveness, 7*, 114–135.

Tipton, E., & Peck, L. (2016). A design-based approach to improve external validity in welfare policy evaluations. *Evaluation Review*. doi:10.1177/0193841X16655656

What Works Clearinghouse. (2014). *WWC procedures and standards handbook, version 3.0*. Retrieved from http://ies.ed.gov/ncee/wwc/pdf/reference_resources/wwc_procedures_v3_0_standards_handbook.pdf

ROBERT B. OLSEN *is an economist and president of Rob Olsen LLC.*

LARRY L. ORR *is an associate at the Bloomberg School of Public Health, The Johns Hopkins University, and an independent evaluation consultant.*

Mead, L. M. (2016). On the "how" of social experiments: Using implementation research to get inside the black box. In L. R. Peck (Ed.), *Social experiments in practice: The what, why, when, where, and how of experimental design & analysis. New Directions for Evaluation, 152,* 73–84.

5

On the "How" of Social Experiments: Using Implementation Research to Get Inside the Black Box

Lawrence M. Mead

Abstract

Implementation research supports impact evaluation by determining how programs have been carried out prior to evaluation, studying what internal features explain high and low performance in a program, and exploring possible new applications of a program model. Permission to interview staff and data availability may limit opportunities for implementation research. Evaluation cannot succeed alone but only as part of a broader process of governmental learning that includes implementation research. © 2016 Wiley Periodicals, Inc., and the American Evaluation Association.

Implementation has proven most difficult in social service programs that seek to promote better outcomes—such as in health, education, or employment—among disadvantaged populations, including welfare mothers, low-skilled men, and school children living in poverty. Such programs seldom produce gains large enough to be reliable without a formal assessment. But for evaluations to be meaningful, inquiry must first be made into how the program has been implemented. In what sense does it exist "on the ground"? To establish *evaluability* is one goal of implementation research. Two other goals are *explanation*, to determine *how* the program produces the effect it does, and *exploration*, or the application of a promising program model to other possible purposes.

This chapter describes how implementation research advances these three goals. I illustrate chiefly with research on welfare employment programs, the area of much of my own research.

The Implementation Problem

Social programs will fail their clients if they are misconceived—or if they are never implemented as intended. Research shows, not surprisingly, that the closer a program adheres to its original design, the better its effects are likely to be (Blakely et al., 1987; O'Donnell, 2008). Implementation often falls short of the ideal. Pilot programs may succeed because they are run by staff that is unusually skilled and dedicated, but when a program is taken to scale staff quality often declines. Teachers in everyday school programs, for example, will typically be less dedicated and well trained than teachers in pilot programs (Chen & Garbe, 2011; Dusenbury, Brannigan, Falco, & Hansen, 2003). One study found that the "treatment strength" of education programs falls by about one standard deviation as programs move from the laboratory to the schools, and this reduces their effectiveness (Hulleman & Cordray, 2009, p. 103).

In the extreme case, a program may not be implemented at all because the agencies in charge never make it a priority (Pressman & Wildavsky, 1984). Or implementation can fail due to diversion of funds or administrative incapacity. A program can fail for technical reasons—it attempts something that simply cannot be done in the field.

Nevertheless, evaluations of social programs commonly ignore this implementation problem. Evaluations can take place with no assurance that the program is actually operating in the way imagined. The proportion of evaluation studies in psychology and psychotherapy that consider implementation seriously is less than half (Moncher & Prinz, 1991), whereas in schools programs, it is less than a quarter (Dane & Schneider, 1998). The likely effect of weak implementation is to bias a program's evaluated impact downward. It also puts the overall validity of the evaluation in question, because the program that is credited with any impacts is so undefined.

Evaluability

One reason implementation is ignored is that analysts' attention typically focuses on the initial design of a program and then on its evaluation—but not on institutional linkages that connect the design to the impact. The roles of bureaucracy and the intergovernmental grant system are usually slighted. Implementation research arose initially in the 1970s to cover this "missing link" in social policy analysis (Hargrove, 1975).

NEW DIRECTIONS FOR EVALUATION • DOI: 10.1002/ev

In evaluability assessment (EA), researchers seek to determine what a program does "on the ground," as against how it was designed to operate. Typical methods include interviews with staff and reviews of program documents and data on the benefits or services delivered. With this data, researchers can determine the program's actual goals and whether its activities serve those ends. Such findings do not establish that the program has impact, that is, that it improves outcomes for clients compared to what would otherwise be. But at least the program exists fully enough so an evaluation can be meaningful (Wholey, 2004).

If implementation totally fails, evaluation would be premature. Rather, policymakers must intervene as "fixers" to clarify who is in charge, make the implementers' task doable, and get the implementers to produce (Bardach, 1977). More often, implementation will be a matter of degree. A program may exist in the sense that it spends money and generates output, but without knowing what it is really trying to do its impact cannot be meaningfully assessed.

In the 1970s, an EA group was established at the Urban Institute in Washington, DC. Its specialty was studying existing social programs in the field to determine what they accomplished in enough detail to permit evaluation. EA is no longer done at the Urban Institute, but it has become a recognized part of research on program effects within the federal bureaucracy as mandated under the Government Performance and Results Act of 1993 and the use of the Program Assessment and Rating Tool since 2002 to appraise programs (D. Rog, personal communication, May 2, 2015).

EA has grown, in part, simply because the use of experimental evaluation has grown. The many evaluations of welfare employment programs by the Manpower Development Research Corporation (MDRC) in the 1980s and 1990s, for example, included detailed descriptions of the programs under study, especially how the programs measured clients' participation. Those results helped interpret the impact findings.

Some implementation research has aimed simply to describe the execution of complex federal programs, without any close tie to evaluation. From the 1970s through the 1990s, Richard Nathan organized implementation studies of several major national policy changes, including the Reagan administration cuts in intergovernmental grants in the 1980s and welfare reform in the 1990s. Local researchers described welfare changes in 21 states using a common plan (Nathan, 1982; Nathan, Doolittle, & Associates, 1983). In the 1990s, an Urban Institute team based in Washington performed similar field studies of welfare reform in 13 states (Zedlewski, Holcomb, & Duke, 1998). (For a summary and analysis of the welfare reform implementation studies, see Mead, 2004b.)

The recent vogue for reinventing government complicates achieving program intentions. Today, successful implementation no longer means simple fidelity to a program design handed down from above. Rather, it means creating an overall bureaucratic system that is efficient and respon-sive to the public. That may not mean executing any one program precisely as dictated (Hill & Hupe, 2002).

Explanation

The second contribution of implementation research is to explain why a program has the effects it has. Assume that a program is effective, better yet that its evaluated impact is favorable. We still cannot explain its perfor-mance. The program usually remains a "black box." We do not know what features make it successful. (For further discussion of this problem, see the Editor's Note and Chapter 6).

With a relatively simple intervention, such as a health treatment or instruction in school, the bureaucratic mechanism that produces effects is relatively clear. To optimize the program, it is enough that fidelity with the intended procedures be high. With more complex programs, however, the linkages between the design and effects are far less clear. To get funding, a program may have to specify very little about how it is organized and run. Then what makes it successful or not remains a mystery, to be discovered only with further research (Gargani & Donaldson, 2011, p. 25).

Impact evaluations tend to analyze and report only average effects (for further discussion, see Chapters 6 and 7). The question is what *variations* in internal policies or operations produce corresponding variations in perfor-mance. In an evaluation, there may be *planned* variation, in the sense that more than one treatment is tested against the control group, to see which has greatest impact. At some sites in the National Evaluation of Welfare-to-Work Strategies (NEWWS), for instance, welfare-to-work programs em-phasizing education or training were compared to other programs stressing quick placement in available jobs; the latter generally showed the largest gains on employment and earnings (Hamilton et al., 2001). Explanatory research, however, aims to uncover *unplanned* variation—differences in pol-icy or operations across sites that were not part of the evaluation design but which researchers think may affect program success.

Alongside the EA group, the Urban Institute in 1975 established a group on implementation research. Its chief projects were studies of the Employment Service (ES), later called the Job Service, a federal–state struc-ture dating back to 1933 designed to help unemployed workers locate jobs, and the Work Incentive (WIN) program, created in 1967 to move employ-able welfare mothers into work. ES was voluntary for its clients, whereas WIN was a mandatory program in which eligible mothers could be re-quired to participate or face cuts in their welfare grants. In both cases, the purpose of research was less to implement the programs—both had been in existence for some time and were well funded—than to optimize their performance.

NEW DIRECTIONS FOR EVALUATION • DOI: 10.1002/ev

Performance Analysis

The ES and WIN studies each took the form of a performance analysis, where the program's own performance measures are modeled using the dimensions that are thought to affect performance, plus control terms. (This section summarizes Mead, 2003.) That is, variation in measured outcomes across sites is related to variation in the features of the sites expected to shape performance, such as local policies or operational differences, while allowing for other, nonprogram factors.

In the ES study, performance was defined as job placements per staff year of program effort. Research focused on states where ES performed well or poorly by this measure relative to what one could expect given the local labor market and the demographics of the clients. Researchers hypothesized that this performance variation would be associated with different styles of organization and management. Field interviewing in these states showed that, indeed, high-performing programs usually had a clearer sense of mission, a flatter bureaucratic hierarchy, and more delegation to the bottom-level staff who directly served the clients than did low-performing programs (Chadwin, Mitchell, Hargrove, & Mead, 1977).

The study of WIN was similar, except that four performance measures were modeled and analyses were done at the level of both state and local programs. Partly due to these differences, findings were more complicated than in the ES study, with several features of bureaucratic and staff quality shown to be associated with high or low performance (Mitchell, Chadwin, & Nightingale, 1980). In both studies, the results were derived from interviews at various levels of the programs and quantitative analysis of program data.

My later studies of WIN and its successor, the Job Opportunities and Basic Skills Training Program (JOBS), followed a similar approach, but my hypothesis then was that performance would vary with the program's ability to require its clients to participate. That idea arose during interviews for the WIN study, when staff reported that obligating mothers to participate was crucial to their going to work. To test that idea, I compared WIN or JOBS offices within New York City, then New York State, then Wisconsin, and also state WIN programs within the nation. In each case, I measured the share of clients who participated (which largely reflected staff requirements to do so) while controlling for variation in other influences such as client demographics and the labor market.

Results confirmed that the participation rate was indeed a strong determinant of the number of job entries a program made. However, the quality of jobs (measured by job entry wage and job retention rate) depended more on the demographics of clients, such as education (Mead, 1983, 1985, 1988, 1997a). The finding that participation strongly shaped job entries was tantamount to finding that results varied with implementation, because the participation rate was itself a measure of implementation.

NEW DIRECTIONS FOR EVALUATION • DOI: 10.1002/ev

Performance Versus Impact

A performance analysis differs from an impact evaluation in several respects. The former shows how a program's measured performance varies from site to site, but it does not establish that the program causes any change compared to no program at all. Comparisons are within the program and not between it and any counterfactual or control group. The unit of analysis is the program, whereas in evaluations, it is usually the individual client.

Also, findings from performance analyses and impact evaluations may differ. That is, features that optimize a program's results in terms of its performance measures may not optimize impacts at the client level. Such a discrepancy has been shown in training programs under the Job Training Partnership Act (JTPA), even though JTPA's performance measures already adjust to some extent for clients' demographics and local labor market conditions (Barnow, 2000; Heckman, Heinrich, & Smith, 1997). This difference between measured performance and impact is likely to be greatest in voluntary programs like JTPA where selection effects can be strong. That is, motivated clients are more likely to participate than unmotivated clients. Motivated clients are likely to do well even without the program. Selection raises measured performance while reducing impact relative to a control group that is also drawn from volunteers. The evaluation will control selection effects, especially if it is experimental. The performance management system, however, may not do so, tempting the program to "cream" and serve mainly the more employable clients.

In mandatory work programs such as WIN or JOBS, however, any divergence of performance from impact appears limited. The program's mandate to participate produces a client pool that needs more help to work than do volunteers, reducing measured performance but raising impact. In turn, performance and evaluation findings tend to run parallel. The performance analyses mentioned above that supported high participation in WIN and JOBS largely confirmed the findings of the early MDRC evaluations of welfare-to-work programs in the same years, showing that the programs that most clearly demanded that clients participate and work generally evaluated best (e.g., Goldman, Friedlander, & Long, 1986; Hamilton & Friedlander, 1989). An unusual analysis that related individual-level impact findings to program features confirmed the main findings of the performance research—welfare-to-work programs perform best even in impact terms if they promote rapid engagement of clients and work over training (Bloom, Hill, & Riccio, 2003). Performance and impact results also showed that enforcing work made it far easier to raise work levels than job quality.

Also, evaluation methodology tends to focus on internal validity. The main goal is to control for nonprogram influences—ideally through experimentation. Only then can gains in outcomes be attributed to the tested program and not to unmeasured attributes of the clients or the setting. But there can be doubt about external validity (See Chapters 3 and 4 in this issue). Even if a program shows impact at one locality, how does one know that it would do the same elsewhere, where social and economic conditions may differ (Greenberg, Meyer, & Wiseman, 1994)? Performance analysis, however, compares results across many sites, so it can be more robust in these terms, even if there is doubt about how well the findings align with impacts.

Finally, although evaluation findings may be more rigorous, performance findings may be more useful to government for improving programs. Operators running local programs typically fear impact assessments because they express a definitive judgment while saying little about what produces the results and how to improve them. Performance findings are more transparent and constructive because more is learned about what produces results and what might optimize them (Chen & Garbe, 2011; Weiss, 1972).

Practical Limitations

One practical limitation of performance analysis is getting clearance from program officials to interview program staff. If the purposes of the inquiry seem too sensitive, access may be denied. The authors of the performance studies mentioned previously obtained clearance because federal and state program executives decided that the findings could improve their programs.

Another problem is data availability. The studies of ES and WIN were feasible in large part because both programs had elaborate reporting systems that covered not only the performance measures but also the demographics of clients and their assignments within the program. Having these data allowed statistical models to be built that related performance measures to both client features and program practices at the local as well as state and national levels. JOBS, which succeeded WIN, had more limited reporting, and since dramatic reform of family welfare in 1996, reporting on welfare-to-work programs has been more limited still.

Several scholars have produced performance analyses using hierarchical modeling, where determinants at both the individual and site levels are combined. These studies therefore include more information than program-based studies and are in principle superior. But the data demands are even greater and seldom met (Bloom, Hill, & Riccio, 2003; Dorsett & Robins, 2013; Godfrey & Yoshikawa, 2012; Heinrich, 2000; Heinrich & Lynn, 2001). As a result, it is likely that performance analyses will continue to be specified chiefly at the program level, where they are possible at all.

Exploration

A third role of implementation research is exploration—to generate new ideas for programs worth studying. Evaluation presumes that we already have a program that is likely to show impact if tested, but how do such programs arise? (See also Chapter 2 in this issue). Analysts devote little attention to this process. Initial program development is often quite unsystematic. Sometimes local program staffs come up with ideas based on earlier programs that disappointed them. Such was the origin of many of the successful local welfare-to-work programs that led to welfare reform (Mead, 2015). In other cases, entrepreneurs were able to fund and implement their own ideas for improved programs based on little more than hunches. Some but not all of these ventures then evaluated well (Price, 2014; Tough, 2008; Whitman, 2008).

Implementation research can bring needed structure to this haphazard process. It provides what is most often lacking in program development—a systematic earlier inquiry. As researchers pursue evaluability and explanation, they learn how a program generates its effects and how it influences its clients enough to guide or improve their lives in any way. Researchers discover this especially through observing program operations in the field and talking with staff.

In exploration, one imagines how a program that succeeds at one purpose could also achieve another. In welfare reform, for example, the success of mandatory work programs gave rise to a general model of antipoverty programming known as paternalism. The idea was that, to succeed, programs for poor people must be supportive but also directive in character. Programs should provide needed benefits and opportunities but also tell their clients clearly what they are supposed to do, such as work or get through school. More than this, the programs should closely supervise their clients to be sure the clients actually fulfill these expectations.

This model appeared in welfare-to-work programs that were especially visible and successful, as in Kenosha, WI, and Riverside, CA (Bardach, 1993; Mead, 2004a). Experts and researchers in education, teen parenthood, homelessness, child support, and drug addiction applied similar insights to their own specialties. In all these areas, programs that combined direction with close supervision appeared to evaluate well or, at least, offer promise (Mead, 1997b).

In evaluation and also EA, researchers presume to know what the preferred program model is. In explanatory research, researchers at least have hypotheses about what factors promote success. In exploratory work, they adopt a more passive stance. They seek to tap the inner wisdom of a program. They ask what efforts officials and other stakeholders have made to solve their own problems (Chen & Garbe, 2011; Van de Ven 2007). What is their "program model," what does it achieve, and could it be applied elsewhere (Gargani & Donaldson, 2011, pp. 25–26)?

The paternalist model arose in just this way. It existed "on the ground" before researchers discovered it—and then generalized from it. Another example is the military approach to education. For decades, the armed forces have seemed to succeed at training youth, even the disadvantaged, in skills needed for military service and later for success in civilian life. Programs set clear standards while providing strong feedback about results and special help for recruits who need it. Only recently has that approach been applied to schools and training programs outside the military (Price, 2014). In still another example, states and localities have begun to develop work programs aimed at low-income men who owe child support or are leaving prison on parole. States and localities have done this with little expert guidance or even knowledge, but now researchers and Washington officials are seeking to develop these programs for wider implementation (Mead, 2011).

Policy Learning

Overall, implementation research has been less prominent recently than it was several decades ago. The complicated intergovernmental grant programs that first raised alarms about implementation in the 1960s and 1970s are today less in question. Antipoverty efforts center more on the larger education, training, and welfare programs, where sheer service delivery is less in question and the main analytic challenge is to determine impact. So implementation research occurs today mainly to describe current programs and establish evaluability.

Also, the very success of impact evaluation in welfare-to-work programs and related areas eclipsed implementation, at least temporarily. MDRC and other evaluators proved that "gold standard" experimental trials could be carried out in regular social programs, not just in laboratories or demonstration projects. Such studies played a pivotal role in welfare reform by establishing that work programs could have largely favorable effects on clients (Weaver, 2000). That gave policymakers enough to chew on for some time.

Some evaluators now think that a "learning community" could be built entirely around impact evaluation. It would gauge the impact of current programs, improve them in light of the findings, and then evaluate them again (Gueron & Rolston, 2013). A gospel of "evidence-based policymaking" built on evaluation may be spreading in Washington (Haskins & Margolis, 2015). The establishment of the Institute of Education Sciences within the federal Department of Education in 2002 was one sign of this. If policy learning chiefly means evaluation, implementation research would be confined entirely to its evaluability role.

That vision overreaches. It shortchanges the broader policy learning by which government improves over time. That process is not systematic, but it is effective and crucial to developing the promising programs that must exist before evaluation can be meaningful. Too much stress on evaluation overlooks the need to optimize existing programs in performance terms, which is far more practical in the short run than impact trials. It neglects the need to extrapolate from "what works" now to what might work better in future. In all these roles, implementation research of one kind or another must come ahead of impact evaluation (Mead, 2015). Evaluation and implementation research are really interactive, with each building upon the other.

References

Bardach, E. (1977). *The implementation game: What happens after a bill becomes a law.* Cambridge, MA: MIT Press.

Bardach, E. (1993). *Improving the productivity of JOBS programs.* New York: MDRC.

Barnow, B. S. (2000). Exploring the relationship between performance management and program impact: A case study of the Job Training Partnership Act. *Journal of Policy Analysis and Management, 19,* 118–141.

Blakely, C. H., Mayer, J. P., Gottschalk, R. G., Schmitt, N., & Davidson, W. S. (1987). The fidelity-adaptation debate: Implications for the implementation of public sector social programs. *American Journal of Community Psychology, 15,* 255–268.

Bloom, H. S., Hill, C. J., & Riccio, J. (2003). Linking program implementation and effectiveness: Lessons from a pooled sample of welfare-to-work experiments. *Journal of Policy Analysis and Management, 22,* 551–575.

Chadwin, M. L., Mitchell, J. J., Hargrove, E. C., & Mead, L. M. (1977). *The Employment Service: An institutional analysis* (R&D Monograph No. 51). Washington, DC: U.S. Department of Labor, Employment and Training Administration.

Chen, H. T., & Garbe, P. (2011). Assessing program outcomes from the bottom-up approach: An innovative perspective to outcome evaluation. In H. T. Chen, S. I. Donaldson, & M. M. Mark (Eds.), *New Directions for Evaluation: No. 130. Advancing validity in outcome evaluation: Theory and practice* (pp. 93–106). San Francisco, CA: Jossey-Bass. doi:10.1002/ev.368

Dane, A. V., & Schneider, B. H. (1998). Program integrity in primacy and early secondary prevention: Are implementation effects out of control? *Clinical Psychology Review, 18,* 23–45.

Dorsett, R., & Robins, P. K. (2013). A multilevel analysis of the impacts of services provided by the U.K. Employment Retention and Advancement Demonstration. *Evaluation Review, 37,* 63–108.

Dusenbury, L., Brannigan, R., Falco, M., & Hansen, W. B. (2003). A review of research on fidelity of implementation: Implications for drug abuse prevention in school settings. *Health Education Research, 18,* 237–56.

Gargani, J., & Donaldson, S. I. (2011). What works for whom, where, why, for what, and when? Using evaluation evidence to take action in local contexts. In H. T. Chen, S. I. Donaldson, & M. M. Mark (Eds.), *New Directions for Evaluation: No. 130. Advancing validity in outcome evaluation: Theory and practice* (pp. 17–30). San Francisco, CA: Jossey-Bass.

Godfrey, E. B., & Yoshikawa, H. (2012). Caseworker-recipient interaction: Welfare office differences, economic trajectories, and child outcomes. *Child Development, 83,* 1382–1398.

Goldman, B., Friedlander, D., & Long, D. (1986). *Final report on the San Diego Job Search and Work Experience Demonstration.* New York: MDRC.

Greenberg, D., Meyer, R., & Wiseman, M. (1994). When one demonstration site is not enough. *Focus, 16,* 15–20.

Gueron, J. M., & Rolston, H. (2013). *Fighting for reliable evidence.* New York: Russell Sage.

Hamilton, G., Freedman, S., Gennetian, L., Michalopoulos, C., Walter, J., Adams-Ciardullo, D., ... Ricchetti, B. (2001). *National Evaluation of Welfare-to-Work Strategies: How effective are different welfare-to-work approaches? Five-year adult and child impacts for eleven programs.* New York: MDRC.

Hamilton, G., & Friedlander, D. (1989). *Final report on the Saturation Work Initiative Model in San Diego*. New York: MDRC.

Hargrove, E. C. (1975). *The missing link: The study of the implementation of social policy*. Washington, DC: Urban Institute.

Haskins, R., & Margolis, G. (2015). *Show me the evidence: Obama's fight for rigor and results in social policy*. Washington, DC: Brookings.

Heckman, J., Heinrich, C., & Smith, J. (1997). Assessing the performance of performance standards in public bureaucracies. *American Economic Review, 87*, 389–395.

Heinrich, C. J. (2000). Organizational form and performance: An empirical investigation of nonprofit and for-profit job-training service providers. *Journal of Policy Analysis and Management, 19*, 233–261.

Heinrich, C. J., & Lynn, L. E., Jr. (2001). Means and ends: A comparative study of empirical methods for investigating governance and performance. *Journal of Public Administration Research and Theory, 11*, 109–138.

Hill, M., & Hupe, P. (2002). *Implementing public policy: Governance in theory and practice*. London, UK: Sage.

Hulleman, C. S., & Cordray, D. S. (2009). Moving from the lab to the field: The role of fidelity and achieved relative intervention strength. *Journal of Research on Educational Effectiveness, 2*, 88–110.

Mead, L. M. (1983). Expectations and welfare work: WIN in New York City. *Policy Studies Review, 2*, 648–662.

Mead, L. M. (1985). Expectations and welfare work: WIN in New York State. *Polity, 18*, 224–252.

Mead, L. M. (1988). The potential for work enforcement: A study of WIN. *Journal of Policy Analysis and Management, 7*, 264–288.

Mead, L. M. (1997a). Optimizing JOBS: Evaluation versus administration. *Public Administration Review, 57*, 113–123.

Mead, L. M. (Ed.). (1997b). *The new paternalism: Supervisory approaches to poverty*. Washington, DC: Brookings.

Mead, L. M. (2003). Performance analysis. In M. C. Lennon and T. Corbett (Eds.), *Policy into action: Implementation research and welfare reform* (pp. 107–144). Washington, DC: Urban Institute.

Mead, L. M. (2004a). *Government matters: Welfare reform in Wisconsin*. Princeton, NJ: Princeton University Press.

Mead, L. M. (2004b). State political culture and welfare reform. *Policy Studies Journal, 32*, 271–296.

Mead, L. M. (2011). *Expanding work programs for poor men*. Washington, DC: AEI Press.

Mead, L. M. (2015). Only connect: Why government often ignores research. *Policy Sciences, 48*, 257–272.

Mitchell, J. J., Chadwin, M. L., & Nightingale, D. S. (1980). *Implementing welfare-employment programs: An institutional analysis of the Work Incentive (WIN) Program* (R&D Monograph 78). Washington, DC: U.S. Department of Labor, Employment and Training Administration.

Moncher, F. J., & Prinz, R. J. (1991). Treatment fidelity in outcome studies. *Clinical Psychology Review, 11*, 247–266.

Nathan, R. P. (1982). The methodology of field network evaluation studies. In W. Williams (Ed.), *Studying implementation: Methodological and administrative issues* (pp. 73–99). Chatham, NJ: Chatham House.

Nathan, R., Doolittle, F. C., & Associates. (1983). *The consequences of cuts: The effects of the Reagan domestic program on state and local government*. Princeton, NJ: Princeton University Press.

O'Donnell, C. L. (2008). Defining, conceptualizing, and measuring fidelity of implementation and its relationship to outcomes in K–12 curriculum intervention research. *Review of Educational Research, 78*, 33–84.

Pressman, J. L., & Wildavsky, A. (1984). *Implementation* (3rd ed.). Berkeley, CA: University of California Press.

Price, H. B. (2014). *Strugglers into strivers: What the military can teach us about how young people learn and grow.* Amherst, MA: Small Batch Books.

Tough, P. (2008). *Whatever it takes: Geoffrey Canada's quest to change Harlem and America.* Boston: Houghton Mifflin.

Van de Ven, A. H. (2007). *Engaged scholarship: A guide for organizational and social research.* Oxford, UK: Oxford University Press.

Weaver, R. K. (2000). *Ending welfare as we know it.* Washington, DC: Brookings.

Weiss, C. H. (1972). *Evaluation research: Methods of assessing program effectiveness.* Englewood Cliffs, NJ: Prentice-Hall.

Whitman, D. (2008). *Sweating the small stuff: Inner-city schools and the new paternalism.* Washington, DC: Thomas B. Fordham Institute.

Wholey, J. S. (2004). Evaluability assessment. In J. S. Wholey, H. P. Hatry, & K. E. Newcomer (Eds.), *Handbook of practical program evaluation* (2nd ed., pp. 33–62). San Francisco, CA: Jossey-Bass.

Zedlewski, S. R., Holcomb, P. A., & Duke, A.-E. (1998). *Cash assistance in transition: The story of 13 states.* Washington, DC: Urban Institute.

LAWRENCE M. MEAD *is a professor of politics and public policy at New York University.*

Peck, L. R. (2016). On the "how" of social experiments: Analytic strategies for getting inside the black box. In L. R. Peck (Ed.), *Social experiments in practice: The what, why, when, where, and how of experimental design & analysis. New Directions for Evaluation, 152*, 85–96.

6

On the "How" of Social Experiments: Analytic Strategies for Getting Inside the Black Box

Laura R. Peck

Abstract

Analysis of postrandom assignment (endogenous) events or experiences in experimental evaluation data is becoming increasingly widespread. This chapter highlights some analytic strategies for revealing mediators of program impacts. In particular, it considers the kinds of research questions that instrumental variables (IV) estimation is suited to answer and how using IV in conjunction with a randomized experiment can advance what we know about the mediational effects of policies or programs. It also explains how the Analysis of Symmetrically Predicted Endogenous Subgroups (ASPES) can assist in answering other, related kinds of evaluation questions. It illustrates how these approaches have been used in practice with an example from the Moving to Opportunity (MTO) Demonstration. © 2016 Wiley Periodicals, Inc., and the American Evaluation Association.

P olicy evaluation is interested in understanding not just *average* treatment effects but the mechanism through which those impacts arise. These mechanisms, or "mediators" that include postrandom-assignment events or experiences—such as participation patterns/dosage—are commonly analyzed using descriptive approaches; but some techniques—the focus of this chapter—build on the experimental design in order to improve the strength of results. Two companion chapters in this issue consider implementation research and design-based approaches for getting inside the black box, with this one focusing on post-hoc analytic strategies. Specifically, this chapter discusses the use of instrumental variable (IV) estimation when applied to experimental data, and the analysis of symmetrically predicted endogenous subgroups (ASPES), including the use of cluster analytic methods for defining endogenous subgroups. The chapter also connects the analytic methods via a common conceptual framework, that of "principal stratification." These approaches can help us learn more about how program-level mediators (such as components of a multifaceted treatment) and individual-level mediators (such as factors in a participant's ecosystem) drive program impacts. For example, regarding program services: What is the effect of providing intensive case management as part of package of program services? Or, considering individual-level mediators, we might ask: What is the effect of earning a credential as part of one's training?

Although more commonly used on existing evaluation data, the analytic approaches that this chapter discusses can be anticipated and are increasingly being planned into evaluations (e.g., by ensuring that the study is adequately powered and that sufficient data are collected to perform the planned analyses; e.g., see Peck, 2015a). The chapter considers which of these approaches are suited to varied social welfare policies and program examples.

The Problem

The comparison of mean outcomes from randomized treatment and control groups reveals the *average* treatment effect, but sometimes other questions are of interest. Specifically of interest is the impact of program-related mediators—that are observed only after randomization, thereby making them endogenous to the treatment—on outcomes. In the frequent situation where an evaluation did not randomize the mediator of interest, the challenge is to identify the right counterfactual: that is, we cannot directly observe those in a control group who would have experienced the mediator if they had been offered the treatment, because they were not offered the treatment. Often nonexperimental analyses that examine mediator effects are plagued by selection bias, which may result in misleading impact estimates. Instead, analysts may be able to learn more by leveraging the experimental design, when possible, to apply either the IV or ASPES approaches described in this chapter. The design-based approaches in Chapter 7 are in many ways preferable to engaging in post-hoc analysis, but sometimes those design options are not feasible. Analysts may want to use rigorous analytic methods that capitalize on existing experimental data to estimate the impacts of mediators. For example, these analytic approaches can help reveal the impacts of taking up the offer of treatment when compliance is incomplete; or they can help reveal the role of achieving a particular program milestone—such as earning a credential as part of a job training intervention—on generating program impacts.

Possible Solutions: Experimentally Based Methods for Conducting Mediation Analyses

This chapter describes some settings in which both the IV and ASPES approaches are suited to estimating the impacts of an intermediate (mediator) variable on outcomes when that mediator is observed after random assignment in an experimental evaluation. Other analytic methods for understanding mediation effects (e.g., structural equation modeling) are not the topic of this chapter, which focuses on analytic methods that leverage an experimental design to improve causal conclusions.

Instrumental Variables, Part 1: Random Assignment as an Instrument for Participation

The method of IV involves using a proxy variable (an "instrument") in order to estimate a causal effect when a randomized experiment is not feasible or available. When overlaid onto an experimental evaluation design, IV involves using random assignment status as a proxy for participation in the treatment offered. It is most common to use random assignment as an instrument to account for no-shows, individuals assigned to the treatment group who receive none of the intervention (e.g., Bloom, 1984) and also the combined effect of no-shows and crossovers (e.g., Angrist, Imbens, & Rubin, 1996). For random assignment status to be a valid instrument for more nuanced mediators (e.g., estimating the impact on low- and high-implementer subgroups), the assumption that random assignment status affects the outcome of interest only through its effect on the mediator of interest must be plausible. That main assumption, the "exclusion restriction," is reasonable in situations where those who did not show up for the treatment to which they were assigned experienced none of the impact of that treatment and assignment to treatment itself has no direct impact on outcomes or other mediating pathways. Beyond adjusting for no-shows and crossovers, this assumption is usually implausible. For example, in the evaluation of a multifaceted intervention, random assignment status could affect outcomes through a number of different channels: participation in the program at all (take-up), quality of the intervention received, participation in a particular program component or combination of components, etc. Therefore, use of random assignment status as an IV is most plausible when considering the impact of a program on those who take-up the treatment (when those who did not show up can be assumed not to have experienced any benefits from being assigned; that is, adjusting for no-shows).

NEW DIRECTIONS FOR EVALUATION • DOI: 10.1002/ev

Instrumental Variables, Part 2: Random Assignment Interacted with Site Indicators as Instruments for Endogenous Subgroup Traits

A yet underused approach is to use IV in a multisite program evaluation where the instrument (individual-level random assignment status) is interacted with site.[1] In turn, the impact estimates are about the relative influence of endogenous traits. Three variants of this approach appear in the literature. In the first, the interaction is between random assignment status and site indicators. An example of this is Raudenbush, Reardon, and Nomi's (2012) work that interpreted the site-specific IV coefficients as site-average effects of participation in the package of services offered at each site. In the second, the interaction is between random assignment status and some site-level participant experience or characteristic. Duncan, Morris, and Rodrigues (2011) used the approach to leverage the cross-site variation in family income to understand the extent to which income had a causal effect on children's academic achievement. Similarly, research on the Moving to Opportunity (MTO) Demonstration considered the five distinct locations of the intervention to examine cross-variation in the effects of neighborhood on a variety of outcomes (e.g., Kling, Liebman, & Katz, 2007); they interacted the neighborhood poverty rate with random assignment status to create an instrument that would proxy neighborhood quality in analyzing its impacts. In the third variant of this IV approach, the interaction is between random assignment and some program characteristic, which might be common across several sites. The work by Reardon, Unlu, Zhu, and Bloom (2014), which examines the influence of implementation fidelity in a school-based math intervention, is an example of the third. They crafted a site-specific implementation measure and interacted that measure with random assignment status to estimate the effects of implementation fidelity on academic achievement outcomes. Although the IV exclusion restriction is still needed, the strategy of interacting random assignment status with site, or with site-level conditions or participant or program experiences offers an opportunity to consider how site characteristics and program experiences associate with impacts.

Principal Stratification: A Framework that Connects IV and ASPES

The principal stratification framework (Frangakis, & Rubin, 2002) generalizes the case of IV in an experimental design and places it within Rubin's "potential outcomes" framework. In doing so, it highlights that within the treatment group there are strata (or subgroups) that have counterparts in the control group, such that their control group potential outcomes might

---

[1] This discussion does not consider the case of a group-randomized experiment and instead focuses on the situation where there are many sites, within which randomization of individuals to treatment and control groups occurred. —

be compared to their actual treatment group outcomes to identify a subgroup impact; and that within the control group there are strata (or subgroups) that have counterparts in the treatment group, such that their treatment group potential outcomes might be compared to their actual control group outcomes to identify a subgroup impact. These strata allow estimation of impacts for subsets of experimental groups, including compliers, either directly or by making assumptions about the presence or direction of effects for selected subgroups (i.e., that there can be no "defiers"—as they are referenced in the literature—and that there is no impact on always-takers or never-takers whose behavior was not changed by the intervention). Indeed, the work of Bein (2013) makes it clear that the ASPES approach estimates principal effects, making the connection that it is a one-sided variant of a principal-stratification-based analysis.

Analysis of Symmetrically Predicted Endogenous Subgroups for Program- and Personally Defined Mediators

The basic steps to undertake the ASPES approach—where a combination of baseline (exogenous) characteristics are used to form subgroups with a propensity to engage in a postrandom assignment experience—are as follows:

- Within a random subsample of an experimental group, use baseline characteristics to model the probability of subgroup membership within the subsample;[2]
- Apply that same model to the remainder of the experimental sample to identify their "predicted" subgroup likelihood, and choose a threshold for dividing the sample into subgroups;
- Estimate the impact on that predicted subgroup as the difference between the mean outcome for predicted subgroup members within the treatment group and the mean outcome for predicted subgroup members in the control group; and
- Convert impacts estimated for predicted subgroups to represent estimated impacts on "actual" subgroups, given certain assumptions.[3]

---

[2] This first part of the analytic process, which involves using out-of-sample prediction, ensures that predicted subgroups are comparably (and symmetrically) identified in the treatment and control groups. Prior work explains how overfitting arises by not using an external modeling sample (e.g., Harvill, Peck, & Bell, 2013; Peck, 2003) and recent work has examined which of a few possible strategies for carrying out the out-of-sample prediction is best (Abadie, Chingos, & West, 2014).

[3] The analysis produces unbiased impact estimates for the symmetrically predicted subgroups, but the conversion step is necessary to recover the true impacts for actual subgroups (Harvill, Peck, & Bell, 2013). The conversion of these estimates to represent the effect on actual subgroups requires assumptions that are not grounded in the experiment. In particular, the average effect of actual subgroup membership must be

This analytic approach involves using baseline characteristics to create subgroups—symmetrically identified in the treatment and control groups—that are associated with some postrandom assignment (endogenous) event or experience. Although the general approach has been more commonly applied, two specific features of the approach—(a) to use a modeling subsample that is distinct from the sample used to estimate impacts[4] and (b) to convert the results from representing impacts on *predicted* subgroups to impact on *actual* subgroups—are unique to the ASPES approach. The first of these ensures that predicted subgroups are symmetric between the treatment and control groups, so that differences in outcomes for these subgroups are unbiased by selection or any other factors that might influence one's choice to follow a given postrandomization path. The second of these means that—when the required conversion assumptions are reasonable (see Bell & Peck, 2013)—the converted impact estimates are also uninfluenced by selection and other sources of bias. It is not the purpose of this chapter to elaborate on the technical mechanics of the approach. Instead, I refer the interested reader to other published research to better understand the mechanics of ASPES (e.g., Bell, & Peck, 2013; Harvill et al., 2013; Peck, 2003, 2013) and provide only this brief introduction here.

This chapter points to ASPES as one of the analytic methods for examining what some refer to as "black box" issues within program evaluation: that there are some experiences that take place within a program that we might like to learn more about and that are endogenous to treatment. ASPES can be useful for understanding two classes of these black box conditions: the first is program mediators, and the second is personally defined mediators. Program mediators are those traits of a program that one might like to learn more about. For example, does being penalized by a welfare program's sanction policy result in different impacts for some specific kinds of individuals? Prior research has considered the sanction policy within a larger, multifaceted welfare reform (e.g., Peck, 2007). A personally defined mediator, in contrast, can include program outputs or intermediate milestones associated with treatment: an individual who achieves a vocational certificate as part of training might be expected to have a different (perhaps more favorable) labor market outcome than someone who does not earn a certificate. In order for ASPES to plausibly estimate the impact of these program and personally defined mediators, baseline variables must have some success in predicting the occurrence of those mediating factors (Peck, 2015a).

---

the same on average for those predicted to be in the subgroup and those predicted not to be in the subgroup (see Bell & Peck, 2013; Peck, 2003). Any application will make this assumption more or less realistic (see Peck & Bell, 2014, for such an application), but using an unbiased treatment effect for predicted subgroups as a starting point has advantages.

[4] The cross-validation approach described in Harvill et al. (2013) permits no sample loss in implementing out-of-sample modeling to avoid overfitting bias.

NEW DIRECTIONS FOR EVALUATION • DOI: 10.1002/ev

Using Cluster Analysis to Identify Complex Subgroups

Although it is straightforward to use the ASPES approach to analyze single, dichotomously defined mediators, the analytic approach can be extended to consider continuously defined and multiple mediators as well as "complexly measured" mediators (as elaborated in Peck, 2015b). These complexly measured mediators reflect experience of a combination of treatment elements and analytic approaches, such as latent class or cluster analysis that can be used for identifying such subgroups. Latent class and cluster analysis are data-driven analyses that reveal relatively homogenous groups within a larger, heterogeneous sample. Gibson (2003) and Peck (2005) used cluster analysis to identify treatment and control group subsets that had particular program-related features. Whether the identifiable types or profiles are meaningful will determine the extent to which this kind of approach is useful for informing policy-relevant questions. Gibson identified several program features, and combinations of features, that characterized certain groups of individuals' program experiences. In doing so, she emphasized their contributions as a "package," with the groupings thereby obscuring the relative effects of *individual* program components, which is what these "black box" opening strategies aim to illuminate. Although using cluster-defined endogenous subgroups may limit usefulness for program design—because it is difficult to parse out the heterogeneity captured in these diverse groups—it may also reflect the reality of programs that offer combinations of features together, not necessarily able to carve them out to stand alone. In response to this recognized limitation, future applications might consider how to focus more clearly on *specific* combinations of program elements that might better open the black box and inform policy decisions and program design.

Illustration: Moving to Opportunity (MTO) Demonstration

The MTO demonstration's experimental evaluation referenced earlier provides a useful example for thinking about the analytic strategies discussed here as possibilities for examining variation in program impacts, specifically that might exist among endogenously-defined strata within the sample. The MTO evaluation randomized public housing residents to a control group or to one of two treatment options: a voucher they could use to move anywhere or a voucher they could use only to move into a neighborhood with low poverty. Researchers were particularly interested in using the experiment to understand "neighborhood effects," which, in observational data, are especially hard to estimate because of the endogeneity of residential choice (i.e., families' choice of where to live and family characteristics, at least in part, influence family outcomes as well as neighborhood conditions).

The main evaluation findings compared the outcomes of those in the treatment groups to the outcomes of those in the control group to estimate an effect of the offer of the vouchers. This is the "intent to treat" (or ITT) impact. Using random assignment as an instrument for participation permits converting those results to represent the impact of the "treatment on the treated" (or the TOT impact) if the exclusion restriction is satisfied (i.e., if the intervention affects an outcome of interest only through its impact on moving with a voucher). Some research has tried to capitalize further on MTO's experimental evaluation design to understand the mediating effect of neighborhood quality on, for example, educational outcomes (Sanbonmatsu, Kling, Duncan, & Brooks-Gunn, 2006), health outcomes (Moulton, Peck, & Dillman, 2014), children's cognitive and behavioral outcomes (Kling, Liebman, & Katz, 2007), family earnings outcomes (Chetty, Hendren, & Katz, 2015), and crime (e.g., Kling et al., 2007). Although not applied to date, the use of cluster analysis to identify certain kinds of individuals within the MTO experimental sample might be promising: the sample is quite heterogeneous, and various kinds of program-related and personally defined mediators might be revealed through use of this approach to subgroup identification. For example, we might be interested to know about how the intervention influenced the outcomes of those who used their voucher to move to a low-poverty neighborhood and whose children attended public school, avoided criminal activity and earned above average grades.

As summarized in Table 6.1, some extensions of the MTO impact analysis used IV alone to estimate the TOT effects (e.g., U.S. Department of Housing and Urban Development, 2011), IV interacted with site detail (e.g., Kling et al., 2007), and ASPES (Moulton et al., 2014) to answer their respective questions about variation in treatment effects. These analyses were undertaken in part because, overall, the evaluation's results were "disappointing." The treatment groups were very heterogeneous, and the demonstration's intent was to learn something about neighborhood effects, but the intervention did not induce as large a change as expected, and so any neighborhood effects that exist were diluted. Within the experimental sample, some people took up the offer of treatment and moved while others did not. Further, among those who moved, some stayed in low-poverty neighborhoods for long periods, whereas others moved to moderate or back to high-poverty neighborhoods after having moved.[5] Trying to understand the mechanisms through which a multifaceted treatment such as MTO had its effects compels using advanced analytic methods, ideally that leverage the strengths of the evaluation's experimental design.

---

[5] Descriptive analyses of these findings appear in work by the Urban Institute (e.g., Turner, Nichols, & Comey, 2012).

Table 6.1. Black Box Analyses of the MTO Demonstration

Research question	Type of analysis	Sample application	Findings/interpretation
What was the impact of being assigned to treatment?	Intent to Treat (ITT) Impact	Evaluation's interim and long-term findings reports: Orr et al. (2003); U.S. Department of Housing and Urban Development (2011)	Being assigned to the experimental treatment group reduced the average neighborhood poverty by 8.0 percentage points (about a 21% reduction relative to the control group mean of 38.6%; Orr et al., 2003, p. 42)
What was the impact on those who took up the offer of treatment?	Treatment on the Treated (TOT) Impact (random assignment status as an IV)		Leasing up within the treatment group (and about half of them did) resulted in living in neighborhoods with 17.2 percentage points *lower* poverty rate, more than a 50% relative reduction from the control group mean (Orr et al., 2003, p. 42).
To what extent did variation in poverty rates (as observed in each study location) affect program impacts?	IV analysis where random assignment status interacts with site to construct an instrument for the effect of neighborhood conditions	Kling, Liebman, & Katz (2007)	Neighborhood poverty rates were more influential on outcomes than assignment to treatment, implying that changing neighborhood conditions (rather than moving to a low-poverty neighborhood) is the trigger driving change.
To what extent did longer exposure to low-poverty neighborhoods affect outcomes?	Analysis of Symmetrically Predicted Endogenous Subgroups (ASPES)	Moulton, Peck, & Dillman (2014)	Spending more time in "low-poverty" (or "high-quality") neighborhoods associates with more favorable health impacts.

Conclusion

A growing literature considers the technical aspects of the analytic approaches described here. I refer the reader to that work for explicit instruction in carrying out an analysis using IV or ASPES to understand the effects of some endogenous subgroup within a larger, experimental sample. Instead, it is the intent of this chapter to highlight the relative potential contributions of some selected analytic approaches to opening up the black box to learn more about the mediational effects of postrandomization events or experiences. Although purely nonexperimental analyses are commonly used for answering these questions, the approaches discussed in this chapter leverage the strength of an experimental evaluation design to improve the credibility of analytic results. IV estimation, when coupled with an experimental evaluation, can involve using random assignment status alone or interacted with site indicators or other variables associated with site in order to understand how a program led to any observed impacts. Likewise, the ASPES uses randomization-induced exogenous variation to identify subsets of an experimental sample whose outcomes can be compared, to reveal the differential impact of treatments in the endogenously defined subgroup. The rigorous analytic tools discussed here offer a promising avenue for helping researchers and policymakers learn more from experiments.

References

Abadie, A., Chingos, M. W., & West, M. R. (2014). *Endogenous stratification in randomized experiments.* Cambridge, MA: Harvard University. Retrieved from http://www.ksg.harvard.edu/fs/aabadie/stratification.pdf

Angrist, J. D., Imbens, G. W., & Rubin, D. B. (1996). Identification of causal effects using instrumental variables. *Journal of the American Statistical Association, 91,* 444–455. doi:10.2307/2291629

Bein, E. (2013, November 7). *Proxy variable and other estimators of principal effects.* Presented at the Annual Fall Research Conference of the Association for Public Policy Analysis and Management, Washington, DC.

Bell, S. H., & Peck, L. R. (2013). Using symmetric predication of endogenous subgroups for causal inferences about program effects under robust assumptions: Part two of a method note in three parts. *American Journal of Evaluation, 34,* 413–426. doi:10.1177/1098214013489338

Bloom, H. S. (1984). Accounting for no-shows in experimental evaluation designs. *Evaluation Review, 8,* 225–246.

Chetty, R., Hendren, N., & Katz, L. F. (2015). The effects of exposure to better neighborhoods on children: New evidence from the moving to opportunity experiment. Cambridge, MA: Harvard University and National Bureau of Economic Research. Retrieved from http://scholar.harvard.edu/files/hendren/files/mto_paper.pdf

Duncan, G. J., Morris, P., & Rodrigues, C. (2011). Does money really matter? Estimating impacts of family income on young children's achievement with data from random assignment experiments. *Developmental Psychology, 47,* 1263–1279.

Frangakis, C. E., & Rubin, D. B. (2002). Principal stratification in causal inference. *Biometrics, 58,* 21–29.

Gibson, C. M. (2003). Privileging the participant: The importance of subgroup analysis in social welfare evaluations. *American Journal of Evaluation, 24*, 443–469. doi:10.1177/109821400302400403

Harvill, E. L., Peck, L. R., & Bell, S. H. (2013). On overfitting in analysis of symmetrically predicted endogenous subgroups from randomized experimental samples: Part three of a method note in three parts. *American Journal of Evaluation, 34*, 545–556. doi:10.1177/1098214013503201

Kling, J. R., Liebman, J. B., & Katz, L. F. (2007). Experimental analysis of neighborhood effects. *Econometrica, 75*, 83–119.

Moulton, S., Peck, L. R., & Dillman, K. (2014). Moving to Opportunity's impact on health and well-being among high dosage participants. *Housing Policy Debate, 24*, 415–446. doi:10.1080/10511482.2013.875051

Orr, L., Feins, J. D., Jacob, R., Beecroft, E., Sanbonmatsu, L., Katz, L. F., ... Kling, J. R. (2003). *Moving to Opportunity: Interim impacts evaluation.* Washington, DC: U.S. Department of Housing and Urban Development.

Peck, L. R. (2003). Subgroup analysis in social experiments: Measuring program impacts based on post treatment choice. *American Journal of Evaluation, 24*, 157–187. doi:10.1016/S1098-2140(03)00031-6

Peck, L. R. (2005). Using cluster analysis in program evaluation. *Evaluation Review, 29*, 178–196. doi:10.1177/01933841X04266335

Peck, L. R. (2007). What are the effects of welfare sanction policies? Or, using propensity scores as a subgroup indicator to learn more from social experiments. *American Journal of Evaluation, 28*, 256–274. doi:10.1177/1098214007304129

Peck, L. R. (2013). On analysis of symmetrically-predicted endogenous subgroups: Part one of a method note in three parts. *American Journal of Evaluation, 34*, 225–236. doi:10.1177/1098214013481666

Peck, L. R. (2015a). Conditions for effective application of analyses of symmetrically-predicted endogenous subgroups. *American Journal of Evaluation, 36*, 532–546. doi:10.1177/1098214015600514

Peck, L. R. (2015b). Using impact evaluation tools to unpack the black box and learn what works. *Journal of MultiDisciplinary Evaluation, 11*, 54–67.

Peck, L. R., & Bell, S. H. (2014). *The role of program quality in determining head start's impact on child development* (OPRE Report #2014-10). Washington, DC: Office of Planning, Research and Evaluation, Administration for Children and Families, U.S. Department of Health and Human Services.

Raudenbush, S., Reardon, S. F., & Nomi, T. (2012). Statistical analysis for multisite trials using instrumental variables with random coefficients. *Journal of Research on Educational Effectiveness, 5*, 303–332. doi:10.1080/19345747.2012.689610

Reardon, S. F., Unlu, F., Zhu, P., & Bloom, H. (2014). Bias and bias correction in multisite instrumental variables analysis of heterogeneous mediator effects. *Journal of Educational and Behavioral Statistics, 39*, 53–86. doi:10.3102/1076998613512525

Sanbonmatsu, L., Kling, J. R., Duncan, G. J., & Brooks-Gunn, J. (2006). Neighborhoods and academic achievement: Results from the Moving to Opportunity experiment. *Journal of Human Resources, 41*, 649–691.

Turner, M. A., Nichols, A., Comey, J., with Franks, K., & Price, D. (2012). *Benefits of living in high-opportunity neighborhoods: Insights from the Moving to Opportunity Demonstration.* Washington, DC: Urban Institute.

U.S. Department of Housing and Urban Development. (2011). *Moving to Opportunity for Fair Housing Demonstration Program: Final impacts evaluation.* Washington, DC: U.S. Department of Housing and Urban Development, Office of Policy Development and Research.

LAURA R. PECK is a principal scientist at Abt Associates Inc., Social and Economic Policy Division and director of Abt's Research and Evaluation Expertise Center. Dr. Peck specializes in innovative ways to estimate program impacts in experimental and quasi-experimental evaluations, and she applies this to many social safety net programs.

NEW DIRECTIONS FOR EVALUATION • DOI: 10.1002/ev

Bell, S. H., & Peck, L. R. (2016). On the "how" of social experiments: Experimental designs for getting inside the black box. In L. R. Peck (Ed.), *Social experiments in practice: The what, why, when, where, and how of experimental design & analysis. New Directions for Evaluation*, 152, 97–107.

7

On the "How" of Social Experiments: Experimental Designs for Getting Inside the Black Box

Stephen H. Bell, Laura R. Peck

Abstract

Program evaluators generally prefer to use the strongest design available to answer relevant impact questions, reserving analytic strategies for use only as necessary. Although the "simple" treatment versus control experimental design is well understood and widespread in its use, it is our contention that creativity in evaluation design can help answer more nuanced questions regarding what about a program is responsible for its impacts. In response, this chapter discusses several experimental evaluation designs that randomize individuals—including multiarmed, multistage, factorial, and blended designs—to permit estimating impacts for specific policy design features or program elements. We hope that recasting what are some long-standing but underused designs in a new light will motivate their increased use, where appropriate. © 2016 Wiley Periodicals, Inc., and the American Evaluation Association.

Design trumps analysis: Program evaluators generally prefer *designing* their studies to generate reliable answers to their research questions over engaging in complex *post-hoc* analyses to get there (Rubin, 2008). For example, Chapter 4 (Orr and Olsen) describes how studies might be better designed to support generalization of findings. The current chapter considers design options that are preferable to even the best analytic innovations (see Chapter 6, Peck) to get "inside the black box" to determine what program features influence program impacts. Although the design options we discuss for this purpose are not new, they are not as commonly used as might be warranted given the promise they hold for exposing key treatment features that generate larger program impacts. All of the strategies advanced here work from randomizing individuals to treatment and control conditions to provide solid evidence of an intervention's average treatment effect. As valuable as such experiments are, the average treatment effect alone is sometimes unsatisfactory for guiding policymakers and administrators on program improvements—by expanding helpful intervention elements or by eliminating unhelpful elements to reduce program costs.

Our goal here is to heighten the profession's awareness of design strategies that can expand learning about program elements from social experiments. We begin by describing a multiarm experimental design strategy that combines three or more experimental groups in one experiment. This approach is illustrated with several studies: the National Evaluation of Welfare to Work Strategies (NEWWS; Hamilton et al., 2001), the Social Security Administration's Benefit Offset National Demonstration (BOND; Gubits, Lin, Bell, & Judkins, 2014), and the Health Profession Opportunity Grants program (HPOG; Peck et al., 2014). We then present a multistage, sequential experimental design that spreads random assignment over multiple points in time as participants flow through the stages of an intervention. This multistage approach is illustrated with a hypothetical job training example (because, to our knowledge, it has not yet been used in a major social experiment) and noted as a potential component of upcoming HPOG experiments. Finally, we discuss a factorial design that crosses one program feature with another to form a matrix of experimental groups to which cases are randomized, as illustrated by the New Jersey Negative Income Tax Experiment (Munnell, 1986). All of these design options focus on individual randomization as the tool of causal inference, though we recognize that cluster-randomized experiments might also be employed for similar purposes to examine the relative impact of treatment variants.

Multiarm Randomization

Adding a third (or additional) experimental arm to a standard two-arm design is one way to create additional treatment contrasts that can provide insights regarding the effects of alternative treatment options. A three-arm random assignment design (arms A, B, and C) creates three contrasts that each imparts learning about a distinct policy question: how much more (or less) effective is policy A than policy B, policy B than policy C, or policy A than policy C. A four-arm design yields six experimental contrasts informing six policy questions. Gubits, Spellman, Dunton, Brown, and Wood (2013) provide an example of a four-arm design in the Family Options

Study that is evaluating alternative assistance strategies for homeless families. Even larger multiarm designs can be used though these are more difficult to execute.

Three-arm designs, randomizing individuals into the control condition or one of two treatment arms, divide into two groups. The two treatment arms can compare (a) wholly different treatment models to see which does better at achieving a policy objective in the target population or (b) the base version of a given treatment model to an enhanced version of the same intervention that adds a further program component to be tested for its contribution to impact. We refer to these two approaches as the "competing treatments" design and the "enhanced treatment" design, respectively, and discuss each in turn.

Competing Treatments Design

NEWWS is an example of a multiarm experiment that compares two alternative program models (Hamilton et al., 2001). This evaluation randomized eligible applicants for welfare assistance to a control group or to one of two contrasting treatments. In treatment arm A, individuals had access to welfare assistance based on a labor force attachment (LFA) model, which emphasized "work first." In treatment arm B, individuals had access to welfare assistance based on a human capital development (HCD) model, which provided education and training as the pathway to better labor market outcomes. Each of the many local welfare offices that implemented the study operated both programs plus a control group, C, that did not receive any welfare-to-work assistance. This allowed the study to assess whether either program model improved on the status quo (A versus C, B versus C) as well as whether the impact of the two approaches differed from one another (A versus B). A head-to-head test of program models of this sort gets inside the black box by allowing comparison of one program model to another program model to discern which might be better at achieving the program's goals.

Enhanced Treatment Design

Another option for multiarm experiments involves comparing the base version of an intervention to an enhanced version identical to the original but with an added program component. This approach focuses on measuring the contribution of the added component to impact magnitude, given the existence of the other components. The Social Security Administration's (SSA) ongoing BOND study illustrates this approach by contrasting a new way of paying Social Security Disability Insurance (SSDI) benefits in one experimental arm, A, to the same benefit adjustment plus enhanced work incentives counseling in a second experimental arm, A + E, and to a current law control group arm, C, representing standard SSDI payment rules (Gubits et al., 2014). This design allows SSA to learn whether the benefit payment change affects individuals' earnings compared to standard rules (A versus C), whether the payment change with enhanced counseling affects earnings compared to standard rules (A + E versus C), and whether the enhanced counseling itself expands the impact of the payment rules (A + E versus A). This single design—with a shared, statistically efficient sample—addresses three policy questions, providing strong experimental evidence on the size of the overall impact and the contribution to overall impact made by the enhanced counseling component.

Another way to develop an enhanced treatment design is to give each of a set of local program agencies the autonomy to choose an enhancement to its base program that can be accessed via a lottery. With this design, a single experiment that operates in several locations can test multiple enhancements, as is the case with the HPOG Impact Evaluation (Peck et al., 2014). The HPOG program offers career-pathways-based training for healthcare sector careers operated in more than 90 locations by 23 grantees. The evaluation has carved out three specific program enhancements to be added to the base program in some locations for an experimental test. Three grantees are enhancing their base programs by offering facilitated peer support groups, intended to increase program attachment and improve retention. Three other grantees are testing the effect of offering additional financial assistance to people who experience exceptional financial stress, such as the threat of imminent eviction from their homes. An additional five grantees are testing a system for rewarding participants for achieving particular program milestones such as perfect attendance, high grades, or staying in a job for at least 90 days. By randomizing individuals to the base program and to these three program enhancements, the evaluation will be in a position to assess if peer support, emergency assistance, and noncash incentives provide—across its many sites—a meaningful boost to the HPOG program's overall effectiveness in those places where each is adopted.

Role of the Control Group

Because the focus of both the competing treatments and enhanced treatment designs is on the contrast between two intervention arms, one might ask: Is a status quo control group even needed? When testing new intervention strategies, such as those in BOND, or selected enhancements to a basic strategy, as in HPOG, the control benchmark is needed to determine whether either of the two alternatives tested improves on current policy. In other contexts, information on status quo outcomes may not be needed and a two-arm design may be sufficient. For example, if a political commitment exists already to deliver an intervention of some sort (no matter the research results), testing multiple interventions against a status quo control group is not necessary. The Job Search Assistance (JSA) Strategies evaluation for welfare recipients, currently in development by the U.S. Department of Health and Human Services, follows this approach (USDHHS, n.d.). Basic

JSA is currently provided to recipients of Temporary Assistance for Needy Families (TANF) throughout the country and is not being considered for retraction as a federal policy action. The JSA Strategies evaluation seeks to determine whether adding certain program features, such as executive function skills development or more intense job search supports, enhances JSA's effectiveness. Because it is interested in variants of JSA services, the study need not impose on the nation the cost and implementation burden of an "untreated" control group. Greater statistical power can be achieved for the focal comparison between the two treatment variants, for a given total sample size, with this approach.

Sample Allocation in Multiarm Designs

This raises a more general design question that must be addressed by all multiarm experiments: Which impact contrast should get the highest policy priority when allocating the research sample among intervention arms, if the total sample size is fixed? There is no formula for this balancing act, though several considerations exist. First, one should consider the relative importance of the various policy comparisons involved and allocate the largest samples to the two experimental arms that define the pairwise comparison of greatest policy importance. Second, the study designer should consider whether *all logically possible* pairwise comparisons are to be addressed; if not, then arms that contribute to a below-average number of comparisons possibly should receive a below-average sample allocation. Third, experimental arms with higher expected rates of nonparticipation in the assigned intervention may need relatively larger sample sizes because nonparticipation reduces the average policy impact the analysis seeks to discover (necessitating a larger sample to detect it). Finally, if an intervention is expected to increase (reduce) the dispersion of outcomes in the study population, then that arm may need more (less) sample due to its larger (smaller) sampling variance.

Multistage Randomization

Another design that gets inside the black box to examine the relative contributions of program elements involves conducting random assignment at different points in an individual's progression through a multistage intervention. Consider a hypothetical job training intervention for which the "front door" to the treatment is controlled by random assignment and—for individuals assigned to treatment at that point who subsequently reach a specified participation milestone—access to the second phase of the intervention is separately randomized. This multistage experimental design supports analysis of three program impact questions of interest:[1]

---

[1] The questions are stated here in their "intention to treat" (ITT) form concerning the average impact of access to intervention services. The same design allows experimental

- What is the average impact of access to the intervention as a whole for all individuals granted access?
- What would be the average impact of access to the intervention were it reduced to a single phase (Phase 1)?
- How much does the Phase 2 component change the average impact of the intervention for those granted access to that phase?

A simple one-stage, two-arm randomized design would answer the first of these research questions. Buried within this overall impact measure is the answer to the other two policy questions, revealed experimentally only by adding a second random assignment "access gate" prior to Phase 2.

Figure 7.1 illustrates this design. It shows two points of randomization, indicating the distinct research groups formed at each point: The initial point of random assignment creates the Phase 1 treatment (T1) and control (C1) groups. Then, a second randomization applies to Phase 1 treatment group members who reach a milestone for advancing to Phase 2 ($T1_M$). Some of these individuals are randomized to gain access to further program components (T2) and some are not (C2). $T1_N$ represents individuals who do not reach the milestone for advancement to Phase 2.

In this design, the overall impact question is answered by comparing the average outcome of individuals in groups $T1_N$ and T2 to the average outcome of those in the main control group, C1. The design also addresses two questions that decompose this overall effect into its Phase 1 and Phase 2 components. Specifically, one can estimate the effect of Phase 1 activities alone by comparing the average outcome for groups $T1_N$ and C2 combined to the average outcome of group C1. In turn, a measure of the added effect of Phase 2 activities for those who become eligible for that stage arises in comparing the average outcome of group T2 to the average outcome of group C2.

At this writing, the design in Figure 7.1 is being considered for the next round of HPOG grant awards and their evaluation, specifically with respect to on-the-job training (OJT). Because of limited funding, OJT would be made available only through a lottery at Phase 2, for those who demonstrate that they are ready for the opportunity by achieving a Phase 1 milestone (U.S. Department of Health and Human Services, 2015). There are two tradeoffs here. First, the added sample that is not part of a conventional (one-stage) two-arm design—C2, the group that upon completion of Phase 1 is denied access to Phase 2—has to come from somewhere. Some combination of the other samples (C1, $T1_N$, and T2) must get smaller to fit that group within the same overall sample size. Second, the impact analyses that combine *two* treatment group samples (either $T1_N$ and T2 or $T1_N$

---

analysis of the corresponding "treatment on the treated" (TOT) impact questions under the usual TOT assumption of "no effect on treatment group nonparticipants" at each stage of the intervention.

Figure 7.1. Multistage Randomized Evaluation Design

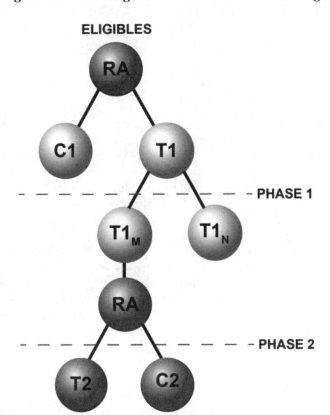

and C2) must do so using analysis weights because the second part of each combined sample is reduced in size by its split between T2 and C2 at the second random assignment point. That is, larger analysis weights must be applied to each of these subsamples than to the $T1_N$ sample with which it is combined to restore the "mix" of participant types to match the mix occurring naturally (without disruption by random assignment) in the main control sample C1.

Both smaller sample sizes and unequal analysis weights increase the standard errors of the resulting impact estimates. As a result, these features of the design make the smallest true overall impact the analysis can confidently detect larger. Work needs to be done to quantify the minimum detectable effect (MDE) tradeoffs among the three research questions listed previously under various sample allocations and to contrast the MDEs achievable here to those addressing each of the same three research questions using the one-stage, three-arm design discussed earlier for achieving the same purposes. Both ways of getting inside the black box have advantages and disadvantages as well compared to the basic one-stage, two-arm design that answers only one research question (the first one) albeit in a statistically more conclusive way. Further work should investigate the optimal sample allocation for aligning a staged randomized design to an evaluation sponsor's policy priorities when multiple impact questions about the black box are posed.

Factorial Designs

In a factorial design, multiple intervention components or "factors"—each with two (or more) levels—are combined in strategic combinations for various randomized samples to answer multiple research questions with statistical efficiency. Examples appear in the literatures on behavioral health, income maintenance, and marketing (e.g., Collins, Murphy, Nair, & Strecher, 2005; Collins et al., 2011; Manzi, 2012; Munnell, 1986). The levels involved can be low versus high dosages of an intervention component or simply its presence versus its absence. Collins et al. (2005) describe the potential goals of a factorial designs as being to determine "which program components are working well; which should be discarded, revised, or replaced; which dosages of program components are most appropriate; whether delivery components are enhancing, maintaining, or diluting intervention efficacy; and whether individual and group characteristics interact with program or delivery components" (pp. 65–66). Clearly, factorial designs may support a much larger learning agenda than designs used to detect an average treatment effect—or even than typical multiarm or sequential randomized designs.

In the simplest form of this approach shown in Figure 7.2 with illustrative sample sizes, a factorial design varies two intervention dimensions or factors in a binary fashion to create four pairwise comparisons. If the levels of each factor are "absence" versus "presence," then both factors absent would define the basic, nonenhanced intervention as shown in the upper left-hand cell of the exhibit. This intervention, with component A added or component B added or both components added, creates the other three cells of the matrix.

Figure 7.2. Illustration of 2×2 Factorial Matrix

		Factor A		
		Absent	**Present**	
Factor B	**Absent**	Basic intervention ($n = 500$)	Basic intervention plus component A ($n = 500$)	$n = 1,000$
	Present	Basic intervention plus component B ($n = 500$)	Basic intervention plus components A and B ($n = 500$)	$n = 1,000$
		$n = 1,000$	$n = 1,000$	$n = 2,000$

In one sense, this design can be considered a four-arm experiment, with an arm for each intervention package shown in the grid. However, by its distinct character this particular four-arm design—factorial in structure—surpasses in statistical efficiency a four-arm design that looks at the marginal contributions of components A and B using an untreated control group arm, an arm with the basic intervention, an arm that adds A to the basic intervention, and an arm that adds B to the basic intervention. It does so by comparing *all* the observations in the second column of Figure 7.2—a "with A" sample of 1,000 total cases—to all the observations in the first column of the exhibit—a "without A" sample of 1,000 total cases. The factorial design similarly supports analysis of the contribution of intervention component B by comparing 1,000 cases in the "with B" second row of the grid with 1,000 "without B" cases in the first row. In contrast, a flat four-arm design is able to isolate the contribution of intervention component A only by comparing samples of 500 (the base-plus-A arm) and 500 (the base arm), and similarly for the contribution of intervention component B.

It should be noted, however, that by pooling pairs of cells the factorial approach measures component A's contribution against a *mixture* of an intervention without component B (the right-to-left comparison in the first row of Figure 7.2) and an intervention with-component B (the right-to-left comparison in the second row of the exhibit). This contrasts with a flat four-way design in which A's contribution is measured against a uniform base intervention containing neither A nor B, albeit with half the sample size. (A similar consideration holds for researching the contribution of component B.) In many contexts, a variegated counterfactual for examining the contribution of a particular program component is no worse than a uniform one, and may be better in that it informs the value of the added component across a range of already existing circumstances.

What is different about a factorial design compared to a "flat" multi-arm design is the added power that comes from increasing the efficiency of the allocation of sample members among the different arms or cells. Specifically, a factorial design offers greater power to detect the impact of a given intervention component because it has a relatively larger "control" group for that factor, which includes all of those randomized not to have access to that component. Shadish, Cook, and Campbell describe a factorial design as one in which "each participant does double duty" (2002, p. 264) by the nature of exposure to particular factors or factor intensities in a crosstab matrix design of the sort shown in Figure 7.2.

In addition to supporting pairwise comparisons of the individual cells in the matrix, factorial designs are configured to estimate the incremental (marginal) impact of each individual factor and the combined impact of the two factors taken together. Contrasts among such findings show whether the two factors combined are synergistic or less than the sum of their parts. Answers to these additional questions do not come with a sample size premium, nor do they diminish the design's power to address the more global

New Directions for Evaluation • DOI: 10.1002/ev

impact questions highlighted previously. As a result, a 2×2 factorial design involving four cells can answer eight questions. A 3×3 design with nine cells answers 16 questions. A "fractional" factorial design—with some cells in the matrix left empty by the sample allocation—will test only a subset of the hypotheses addressed by a fully populated matrix. A well-known application of this design is the New Jersey Negative Income Tax experiment in the late 1960s and early 1970s, which defined income guarantees for families by poverty level (at 50%, 75%, 100%, and 125% of the then poverty line) and the "tax rate" on earnings (at 30%, 50%, and 70%). Although this 4×3 design had 12 potential cells (and the ability to answer *many* policy questions), researchers assigned participants to the eight least expensive and most politically palatable combinations of the two parameters, leaving some cells empty (Kershaw & Fair, 1976).

Conclusion

How can researchers design more ambitious social experiments to learn more from future studies than has typically been learned in the past? This chapter has presented a range of approaches to expand learning when the goal is to measure the contribution of specific features of interventions to overall impacts. The design approaches presented all use random assignment so that resulting evidence is as strong as possible, untainted by selection and other sources of bias. A major goal here is to show that high internal validity of this sort, achieved through experimentation, does not have to be sacrificed to investigate how intervention components contribute uniquely to the magnitude of program impacts. One hope is that the three experimental design strategies in this chapter will position impact evaluators with control over sampling to use randomization more frequently to open the black box and discover what makes programs effective.

References

Collins, L. M., Murphy, S. A., Nair, V. N., & Strecher, V. J. (2005). A strategy for optimizing and evaluating behavioral interventions. *Annals of Behavioral Medicine, 30,* 65–73.

Collins, L. M., Baker, T. B., Mermelstein, R. J., Piper, M. E., Jorenby, D. E., Smith, S. S., ... Fiore, M. C. (2011). The multiphase optimization strategy for engineering effective tobacco use interventions. *Annals of Behavioral Medicine, 41,* 208–226. doi: 10.1007/s12160-010-9253-x

Gubits, D., Lin, W., Bell, S., & Judkins, D. (2014). *BOND implementation and evaluation: First- and second-year snapshot of earnings and benefit impacts for stage 2.* Cambridge, MA: Abt Associates, 2014. Retrieved from http://www.ssa.gov/disabilityresearch/documents/BOND_Deliverable%2024c5_8-14-14.pdf

Gubits, D., Spellman, B., Dunton, L., Brown, S., & Wood, M. (2013). *Interim report: Family Options Study.* Washington, DC: U.S. Department of Housing and Urban Development. Retrieved from http://www.huduser.org/portal/publications/pdf/HUD_503_Family_Options_Study_Interim_Report_v2.pdf

Hamilton, G., Freedman, S., Gennetian, L., Michalopoulos, C., Walter, J., Adams-Ciardullo, D., ... Ahluwalia, S. (with Small, E., & Ricchetti, B.). (2001). *National Evaluation of Welfare-to-Work Strategies: How effective are different welfare-to-work approaches? Five-year adult and child impacts for eleven programs.* Washington, DC: U.S. Department of Health and Human Services, Administration for Children and Families, Office of the Assistant Secretary for Planning and Evaluation and U.S. Department of Education, Office of the Deputy Secretary, Planning and Evaluation Service, Office of Vocational and Adult Education.

Kershaw, D., & Fair, J. (1976). *The New Jersey Income-Maintenance Experiment: Vol. 1. Operations, surveys, and administration.* New York: Academic Press.

Manzi, J. (2012). *Uncontrolled: The surprising payoff of trial-and-error for business, politics, and society.* New York: Basic Books.

Munnell, A. H. (Ed). (1986). *Lessons from the Income Maintenance Experiments.* Conference Series No. 30. Boston, MA: Boston Federal Reserve and Washington, DC: Brookings Institution. Retrieved from https://www.bostonfed.org/economic/conf/conf30/

Peck, L. R., Werner, A., Fountain, A. R., Buell, J. L., Bell, S. H., Harvill, E. L., ... Locke, G. (2014). *Health Profession Opportunity Grants impact study design report* (OPRE Report #2014-62). Washington, DC: Office of Planning, Research and Evaluation, Administration for Children and Families, U.S. Department of Health and Human Services.

Rubin, D. R. (2008). For objective causal inference, design trumps analysis. *The Annals of Applied Statistics, 2,* 808–840. doi:10.1214/08-AOAS187

Shadish, W. R., Cook, T. D., & Campbell, D. T. (2002). *Experimental and quasi-experimental designs for generalized causal inference.* New York: Wadsworth Publishing.

U.S. Department of Health and Human Services, Administration for Children and Families, Office of Planning, Research and Evaluation. (2015). *National and tribal evaluation of the 2nd generation of the Health Profession Opportunity Grants (HPOG)* (Solicitation 15-233-SOL-00191).

U.S. Department of Health and Human Services, Administration for Children and Families, Office of Planning, Research and Evaluation. (n.d.). *Job Search Assistance Evaluation, 2013–2018.* Retrieved from http://www.acf.hhs.gov/programs/opre/research/project/job-search-assistance-evaluation

STEPHEN H. BELL *is a vice president and senior fellow at Abt Associates Inc., Social and Economic Policy Division.*

LAURA R. PECK *is a principal scientist at Abt Associates Inc., Social and Economic Policy Division and director of Abt's Research and Evaluation Expertise Center.*

Maynard, R., Goldstein, N., & Nightingale, D. S. (2016). Program and policy evaluations in practice: Highlights from the federal perspective. In L. R. Peck (Ed.), *Social experiments in practice: The what, why, when, where, and how of experimental design & analysis. New Directions for Evaluation, 152*, 109–135.

8

Program and Policy Evaluations in Practice: Highlights from the Federal Perspective

Rebecca Maynard, Naomi Goldstein, Demetra Smith Nightingale

Abstract

This paper examines the intersection of evaluation methods and usefulness of research for policy and practice from the vantage point of federal agencies that commission a large share of domestic program evaluations with the goal of improving the ability of the government to invest its scarce dollars wisely. Toward this end, the paper revisits the prominent issues discussed in prior chapters through a lens focused on understanding conditions under which particular methodological strategies are and are not helpful in advancing the job of policy analysts, policymakers, and program administrators. The aim is to provide useful guidance to evaluators in how to interact productively with the evaluation funders and intended end-users regarding how they might make their products most useful. © 2016 Wiley Periodicals, Inc., and the American Evaluation Association.

The Role of the Federal Government in Program and Policy Evaluation

Much of the evaluation research on labor, education, and human services in the United States is supported by the Administration for Children and Families (ACF) in the U.S. Department of Health and Human Services, by various offices within the U.S. Department of Labor, and by the Institute of Education Sciences in the U.S. Department of Education. The product of such research is critical to the central missions of these agencies, which include protecting the health, welfare, and economic opportunity of the population through the design, implementation, and management of policies and programs that serve the public interest. For example, as the nation struggles with large numbers of adults who are ill equipped to succeed in today's workforce and have persistently low rates of college completion, the U.S. Department of Education needs reliable evidence to inform its deliberations about programs and policies. These include programs and policies to better prepare young adults for careers and/or college through the K–12 education system, to increase access to college admission for such youth, and to increase the college completion rates of those who do enroll.

The U.S. Department of Labor's mission is to promote the welfare of current, future, and retired workers, including providing opportunities for labor market advancement and protecting workplace health, safety, and labor standards. Its leaders need reliable evidence about the absolute and relative effectiveness of programs and strategies that advance these goals, while also addressing their implications for the businesses and industries that provide jobs. In the same way, the U.S. Department of Health and Human Services needs information on the effectiveness of approaches to support the health and welfare of individuals from birth through adulthood. These include approaches to supporting early child care and education, preventing adolescent pregnancy, and preventing and responding to child abuse and neglect.

Prior chapters in this issue provided an overview of the range of evaluations that have been conducted to support such information needs, highlighting some of their strengths and weaknesses (see especially Rolston, Chapter 1). For example, evaluations commonly use two-group experimental or quasiexperimental designs for estimating program impacts and producing reliable estimates of average per-participant impacts (Murnane & Willette, 2010; Orr, 1999). Generally, these studies are not designed to support rigorous evidence about for whom and under what conditions varied outcomes would be better or worse (Durlak & DuPre, 2008; Fixsen, Naoom, Blasé, Friedman, & Wallace, 2005; Granger & Maynard, 2015; Weiss, Bloom, & Brock, 2014).

The prior chapters outline a range of strategies to align evaluation designs with the priority information needs of the agencies (see especially Bell & Stuart, Chapter 3; Olsen & Orr, Chapter 4; Peck, Chapter 6); explore issues related to the optimal timing of evaluations relative to the status of program design, development, and implementation (Epstein & Klerman, Chapter 2); and reflect on the complementarity of performance analysis, implementation research, and impact evaluations (Mead, Chapter 5). These are all strategies that align well with public and private initiatives to elevate the role of evidence in public policy and funding decisions (Haskins & Baron, 2011; Haskins & Margolis, 2014; Mervis, 2013;

NEW DIRECTIONS FOR EVALUATION • DOI: 10.1002/ev

Nussle & Orszag, 2014) and with the push toward greater integration of improvement science into public administration (Bryk, 2009; Bryk, Gomez, Grunow, & LeMahieu, 2015).

In this final chapter, we explore ways to improve the value of policy and program evaluations from the perspectives of current and former government officials whose professional responsibilities lie at the intersection of producing and using evidence to inform federal policies and overseeing the practices of federally sponsored programs. Specifically, the evidence generated through evaluations can be very important in two policy domains: (a) responsible oversight of federal resources, policies, and programs, and (b) efficient allocation of scarce program dollars. Such evidence is most useful if it is reliable and relevant to the current contexts of policy and practice and if it supports meaningful comparisons across programs or policy options.

Shortcomings of the Evaluation Enterprise

In addition to not answering all of the questions federal decision makers want answered, a number of other shortcomings are inherent in the evaluation enterprise. Evaluation results inevitably reflect the past, whereas their utility is in informing decisions about ongoing program performance or about the future. When long-term outcomes are of interest, this conundrum is especially acute, as the gap in contexts for the evidence and its intended application to inform future policy or practice becomes very large. For example, evidence on persistence of the effects of a preschool intervention through fifth grade or beyond necessarily will be based on data contrasting the lasting effects of preschool experiences that occurred at least 6 years earlier—a sufficient time for substantial changes to occur in the character of both the preschool population and the education context.

Evaluations rarely have sufficient population and setting coverage to be fully generalizable to the range of relevant policy contexts. Rather, studies of promising interventions (e.g., job training programs designed to be offered through community colleges or teacher professional development designed for professional learning communities) must balance the goal of producing credible estimates of program impacts against the often competing goal of producing impact estimates that generalize to a range of settings and population groups (e.g., to training institutions nationwide or to teachers who are and are not part of a formal learning community).

Evaluations often do not attend to issues, such as long-term impacts, that are important for translating the study findings into terms that are useful for performance management. Often program administrators and elected officials want evaluation findings to support immediate decisions about program resources or best practices. Rather, evidence from evaluations is best viewed as cumulating through testing replications and demonstrating promising strategies in various settings. Evaluations could be more useful,

NEW DIRECTIONS FOR EVALUATION • DOI: 10.1002/ev

however, if they were designed to facilitate translation of the findings to support improving performance and performance metrics.

As discussed throughout this issue, diversity in program and policy populations, settings, and contexts means there will always be a multiplicity of questions about generalizability. Moreover, the complexity of many interventions means there will usually be a multiplicity of questions about how sensitive the impacts are to variations in particular elements of the policy or practice. As a consequence, evaluations and their independent findings are a precious resource. For this reason, it is important to be strategic in prioritizing the questions to be addressed, often balancing the breadth of questions against the credibility of the evidence the evaluation will yield for each. The emphasis should be first and foremost on the questions of greatest importance to policymakers and program administrators. Indeed, a necessary but not sufficient condition for evaluation findings to be used by policymakers is that the evaluation address such relevant questions (Daly, Finnigan, Moolenaar, & Che, 2014; Nutley, Davies, & Walter, 2002; Oliver, Innvar, Lorenc, Woodman, & Thomas, 2014; Tseng, 2014).

The evaluation strategies discussed in this issue represent important methodological approaches for increasing the utility of individual studies, conditional on having agreement on the relevance and priority of questions to be addressed. Notably, these expanded and improved methods increase, rather than diminish, the importance of collaboration between the evaluation funders and the evaluators in identifying and prioritizing the questions to be addressed. Too often the policymakers focus on narrow questions of immediate interest when commissioning studies and evaluators either simply service the expressed interests of the funder or enlarge the focus of the study by inserting questions aligned with their personal professional or disciplinary interest. A more meaningful approach would give strong weight both to questions that are expected to have short-term relevance and to those that are likely to be of enduring interest, as well as being sensitive to the nature of the question. For example, some evaluations are motivated by concerns about responsible design and oversight of programs and policies, whereas others are driven by concerns about the efficiency of resource use and the implications for funding priorities.

Responsible Oversight

In the federal context, accountability has many layers. Members of Congress want to know the results of programs they authorize and fund. Within the executive branch, White House policy and budget officials, Cabinet secretaries, subcabinet officials, and program directors all want information on results of government investments and policy decisions. The public—whether as citizens, voters, taxpayers, or interest groups—is interested in the consequences of individual government programs and policies and, sometimes, interested in comparisons with alternatives. Subgroups of the public have a vested interest in federal decisions about what should be evaluated and the results of those evaluations. These subgroups include researchers and evaluators, who count universities, foundations, special interest groups, and state and local governments among their constituencies, as well as advocates and the press. Notably, implementers of federally funded programs (e.g., state and local governments and various community and other nongovernmental organizations) also have their own perspectives on the utility of various types of evaluation and evaluation evidence, which are influenced by their constituencies.

These diverse sectors and groups share an interest in the general question "does it work?" However, that question has many permutations. For example, Congress may be most interested in knowing the overall effect of a program or policy, whereas a federal program director may care more about whether a policy change or technical assistance initiative improved the effectiveness of a program. A special interest group may want to know how well the program served a specific population group or how well it would work in a specific geographic area.

Even constituencies interested in evidence of program effectiveness often are vague or silent on the question of the implied counterfactual in their question: They are not explicit about "compared to what?" even though this matters a lot in terms of the usefulness of the study findings for them. The implications of evaluation findings hinge critically on being clear not only about the qualities of the program or policy being evaluated but also about the counterfactual against which it is being judged.

Evaluations of universal policies that have been enacted present special opportunities and challenges. For example, generally it is not possible to rigorously test the absence of the policy, because that would entail exempting individuals from the policy. However, studies can be designed to yield highly credible and useful information about how to improve such programs or use resources more efficiently. For example, evaluations could be designed to test the relative effectiveness of different approaches to increasing voluntary compliance with labor standards, such as minimum wage and overtime laws or occupational safety and health requirements. The results of such evaluations can identify specific actions the government might take to improve the efficiency of its operations (e.g., by targeting compliance resources on employers or industries that are least likely to voluntarily comply and possibly more likely to be violating the rules). Similarly, programs that have low take-up rates among the intended service recipients could potentially benefit from planned variation impact evaluations testing the effect of different outreach strategies. The results of such studies are immediately relevant to decisions program administrators could make about outreach strategies and investments.

NEW DIRECTIONS FOR EVALUATION • DOI: 10.1002/ev

Efficiency in Resource Use

In recent years, the emphasis on evidence-based decision making has surged throughout government (Haskins & Margolis, 2014; Nussle & Orszag, 2014). The most visible evidence of this is the various federal program initiatives that explicitly condition funding on the level of evidence that the investment will pay off. For example, the statute authorizing the U.S. Department of Health and Human Services's Maternal, Infant, and Early Childhood Home Visiting program (Social Security Act sec. 511 (d)(3)(A)(II)) reserves 75% of grant funds for evidence-based models.

Tiered funding strategies are one way the federal government is directing limited resources to programs and policies that have evidence of their effectiveness. Under these schemes, the largest grant amounts are reserved for applicants proposing to use strategies that have very strong evidence of effectiveness (i.e., those that already have highly credible evidence of effectiveness); lower levels of funds are allocated to successful applicants who have some, but less convincing evidence of effectiveness but who are committing to experimental tests of effectiveness; and the smallest grants are for those who are proposing further development and testing of promising but untested strategies.

For example, the U.S. Department of Education's Investing in Innovation program provides large "scale-up" grants for implementing models with the strongest evaluation evidence, smaller "validation" grants for models with moderate evaluation evidence, and still smaller "development" grants for models with only preliminary evidence (U.S. Department of Education, 2015). The U.S. Department of Labor also has used tiered funding to encourage more experimental design testing within large-scale discretionary grant programs, including the Trade Adjustment Act Community College Career Training Program (TAACCCT) and the multigrant Workforce Innovation Fund (U.S. Department of Labor, 2014, 2015;).

Even when high-quality evaluations are conducted and valued by federal agencies, officials often are hard pressed to determine how to use the evaluation findings due in large part to the exigencies of governance and administration. The more effective evaluators are at anticipating the government's need for information and factoring these needs into study plans, the more likely it is that their evaluations will produce the evidence needed to improve the policymaking and oversight processes.

Challenges Meeting Evidence Needs to Guide Policy Development and Monitoring

Federal agencies face myriad challenges in meeting their needs for reliable evidence to support ongoing program monitoring, program improvement, and new policy development. These include challenges stemming from the nature of the information they require, the timing of when information is useful to them, and the diversity of the audiences for the information. Although program agencies generally have some staff with strong evaluation backgrounds, many agency staff members and the majority of their constituents lack both the technical skills and time to review and effectively apply evidence to their jobs as program administrators, policy analysts, or policymakers. This is especially the case for evidence that is presented in a complex or technical way (Nutley et al., 2002; Tseng, 2012).

Timeliness of Evidence

Many decisions in government are driven by fiscal year planning and election cycles. As agencies commissioning research balance considerations of the immediacy of need, funding availability, and the time and resources required to meet various information needs, they often prefer low-cost evaluations that can be conducted quickly. Most often, program decisions will be made based on reviews of the evidence in hand and, sometimes, on quick turnaround secondary analyses of extant research or program databases. However, occasionally it is feasible to conduct a new evaluation to address information needs within a relatively short period of time or to modify an ongoing evaluation to incorporate new research questions. For example, it would be relatively quick and easy to mount an evaluation to learn about the take-up rate on a new student loan option; it would take much longer to learn what the impact of the policy would be on college graduation rates.

It also would be relatively quick and easy to learn about the impacts of modifying the outreach strategy for an employment or training program on the size and composition of the applicant pool. This would require only varying the recruitment strategies used in different "recruitment zones" and then measuring applications and yields associated with different approaches. The test could be of competing strategies (e.g., blogging, targeted e-mails, and radio ads) or of adding one or more targeted strategies to the standard bundle, with the specific aim of improving outcomes for high mobility groups such as veterans recently separated from active duty. For example, an ongoing quick turnaround evaluation is focusing on the impact of alternative strategies for increasing voluntary requests for the Operational Safety and Health Administration's On-Site Consultation services (see www.osha.gov/consultation). The rationale is that greater experimentation would accelerate the identification and implementation of policies and practices that improve workplace safety and thereby reduce injuries, illness, and fatalities.

Indeed, a quick turnaround evaluation was instrumental in demonstrating that integrating Unemployment Insurance Reemployment Eligibility Assessments with Reemployment Services improved outcomes significantly at little to no added cost (Oates, 2012; Poe-Yamagata et al., 2011). However, this modest change in program practice is only a piece of the puzzle. Only a small share of unemployment recipients use reemployment services and, therefore, the promise of this service integration strategy to reduce the need for Unemployment Insurance depends on whether it is possible to also identify ways of increasing participation in reemployment services.

Access to Reliable Extant Evidence

A major challenge for policymakers is having up-to-date information on what is and is not known about the effectiveness of particular programs, policies, or practices. Even when evidence that would inform particular policy deliberations exists, it often is not readily accessible to those conducting the policy analysis or translating findings into actionable recommendations. Moreover, most intended end users of the evidence lack the time and technical skills to judge the credibility of the evidence and assess its applicability to the target context.

These challenges featured prominently in the rationales for developing evidence clearinghouses, such as the What Works Clearinghouse for education research, the Clearinghouse for Labor Evaluation and Research, the Home Visiting Evidence of Effectiveness Review, and the Teen Pregnancy Prevention Evidence Review. A list of selected clearinghouses appears in Table 8.1. Each of these clearinghouses systematically retrieves, reviews, and disseminates through web-accessible libraries information on the existence, quality, and findings of evaluations of institutionalized programs, as well as pilot and demonstration programs that aim to address important issues of policy and practice. The clearinghouses have many common features and have been influenced by one another. However, they also differ in a number of respects other than in their focal policy area. These differences include the specific criteria they use for judging the credibility of the evidence, the format and content of the summary information they report, and the frequency of and conditions for updating the databases. It also is notable that many studies are included in more than one of these clearinghouses. For example, education interventions, such as Career Academies (Kemple & Willner, 2008), address education and workforce readiness goals and so the study is included in both the Clearinghouse for Labor Evaluation and Research and the What Works Clearinghouse.

These databases have become increasingly valuable to policymakers and practitioners as the federal government has ramped up its emphasis on evidence-based funding of development and scale-up initiatives. In many instances, funding eligibility requires that the applicant provide documentation of a minimum standard of evidence to support the likelihood that the proposed program or policy will have the intended effect. For example, the U.S. Department of Education's Investing in Innovation (i3) program invites applicants to apply for one of three levels of funding, each requiring a specific level of evidence. For this competition, the credibility of the evidence supplied is judged against the What Works Clearinghouse evidence

Table 8.1. Selected Evidence Clearinghouses, 2015

Clearinghouse Name	Sponsoring Agency	Weblink
Clearinghouse for Labor Evaluation and Research (CLEAR)	U.S. Department of Labor	http://clear.dol.gov/
Crime Solutions	Office of Justice Programs	http://www.crimesolutions.gov/
Find Youth Info	The Interagency Working Group on Youth Programs	http://youth.gov/
National Clearinghouse on Families & Youth	National Commission on Families and Youth	http://ncfy.acf.hhs.gov/
Home Visiting Evidence of Effectiveness (HomVEE)	U.S. Department of Health and Human Services, Administration for Children and Families, Office of Planning, Research, and Evaluation	http://homvee.acf.hhs.gov/
Teen Pregnancy Prevention Evidence Review Database	U.S. Department of Health and Human Services	http://tppevidencereview.aspe.hhs.gov/StudyDatabase.aspx
What Works Clearinghouse (WWC)	U.S. Department of Education, Institute of Education Sciences	http://ies.ed.gov/ncee/wwc/
Workforce Systems Strategies	U.S. Department of Labor, Employment and Training Administration	https://strategies.workforcegps.org/

Note: All program weblinks were accessed between October 23, 2015, and July 29, 2016.

standards (U.S. Department of Education, 2015). For this competition in particular, the What Works Clearinghouse is an important "go to" source both to understand what the relevant evidence standards are and to potentially identify studies that provide (or fail to provide) the requisite evidence by searching its database of more than 10,000 reviewed studies (see http://ies.ed.gov/ncee/wwc/ReviewedStudies.aspx).

Similarly, the Maternal, Infant, and Early Childhood Home Visiting program sponsored by the U.S. Department of Health and Human Services relies on the Home Visiting Evidence of Effectiveness Review (http://homvee.acf.hhs.gov/) to determine which home visiting models grantees can support with the 75% of their federal funds that is reserved for evidence-based models. The federal Performance Partnership Pilots for Disconnected Youth (P3) authorized under HR3547 (U.S. Department of Education, 2014) expands the tiered-evidence grant making concept to improve outcomes for disconnected youth (i.e., youth not in school and not working). P3 pilot communities are allowed to blend and braid federal funding from several agencies, including the U.S. Departments of Education, Health and Human Services, and Labor and the Corporation for National and Community Service. Evidence-based criteria were used to select the P3 pilots in accordance with the evidence standards used in the relevant federal agency's evidence-based clearinghouses. Moreover, all evaluations of the P3 initiatives are, in turn, being subjected to the standards of the same evidence clearinghouse. In these and other recent examples (summarized in Table 8.2), the intent is both to adopt strategies with strong evidence of effectiveness and to continue to add to the evidence base through rigorous evaluations of the funded initiatives.

Commissioning New Evaluations

Of course, for some sufficiently persistent priority concerns, the federal government will invest in long-term and often large-scale evaluations. Because some important questions take a long time to answer, federal officials who plan and fund such evaluations must choose questions that are likely to be of lasting interest. Results from an evaluation begun under one administration may well become available only during the subsequent administration. For example, on several occasions, both the U.S. Departments of Labor and Health and Human Services have made major investments in evaluations of the effectiveness of various approaches to improving the self-sufficiency of population groups such as teenage parents, school dropouts, and long-term welfare recipients (see, e.g., Butler et al., 2012; Kemple & Willner, 2008; Schochet, Burghardt, & McConnell, 2008). For programs like Job Corps and Career Academies that intervene during high school with the primary goal of improving the health and social and economic well-being of individuals throughout adulthood, judgments of their success could not be reached without long-term follow-up.

Table 8.2. Illustrative Evidence-Based Programs at the U.S. Departments of Health and Human Services, Labor, and Education

Program, Website	Description
First in the World http://www2.ed.gov/programs/fitw/index.html	The FITW program is designed to support the development, replication, and dissemination of innovative solutions and evidence for what works in addressing persistent and widespread challenges in postsecondary education for students who are at risk for not persisting in and completing postsecondary programs, including, but not limited to, adult learners, working students, part-time students, students from low-income backgrounds, students of color, students with disabilities, and first-generation students.
Investing in Innovation http://www2.ed.gov/programs/innovation/index.html	The Investing in Innovation Fund, established under section 14007 of the American Recovery and Reinvestment Act of 2009 (ARRA), provides funding to support (a) local educational agencies (LEAs) and (b) nonprofit organizations in partnership with (i) one or more LEAs or (ii) a consortium of schools. The purpose of this program is to provide competitive grants to applicants with a record of improving student achievement and attainment in order to expand the implementation of, and investment in, innovative practices that are demonstrated to have an impact on improving student achievement or student growth, closing achievement gaps, decreasing dropout rates, increasing high school graduation rates, or increasing college enrollment and completion rates. These grants will (a) allow eligible entities to expand and develop innovative practices that can serve as models of best practices, (b) allow eligible entities to work in partnership with the private sector and the philanthropic community, and (c) identify and document best practices that can be shared and taken to scale based on demonstrated success.
Maternal, Infant, and Early Childhood Home Visiting Program http://mchb.hrsa.gov/programs/homevisiting/	Health Resources and Services Administration (HRSA), in close partnership with the Administration for Children and Families (ACF), funds states, territories, and tribal entities to develop and implement voluntary, evidence-based home visiting programs using models that are proven to improve child health and to be cost effective. These programs improve maternal and child health, prevent child abuse and neglect, encourage positive parenting, and promote child development and school readiness.

(Continued)

Table 8.2. Continued

Program, Website	Description
Social Innovation Fund http://www.nationalservice.gov/programs/social-innovation-fund/about-sif	Authorized by the Edward M. Kennedy Serve America Act in April 2009, the Social Innovation Fund is a program of the Corporation for National and Community Service (CNCS), a federal agency focused on improving lives, strengthening communities, and fostering civic engagement through service and volunteering. Together, service and innovation provide a vehicle to harness the power of ordinary people and unleash the potential of innovative ideas to help address our communities' toughest social problems and transform lives. The Social Innovation Fund's (SIF's) portfolio represents $241 million in federal grants and more than $516 million in nonfederal match commitments. To date, the SIF's Classic program has awarded 27 grant-making organizations and 189 nonprofits working in 37 states and the District of Columbia. The 189 nonprofit organizations being funded are conducting 73 interventions and evaluating results through highly rigorous models. Through the SIF's Pay for Success program, over 30 jurisdictions across the United States are engaged in testing and implementing Pay for Success projects.
Trade Adjustment Assistance Community College and Career Training http://doleta.gov/taaccct/	In 2009, the American Recovery and Reinvestment Act amended the Trade Act of 1974 to authorize the Trade Adjustment Assistance Community College and Career Training (TAACCCT) Grant Program. On March 30, 2010, President Barack Obama signed the Health Care and Education Reconciliation Act, which included $2 billion over 4 years to fund the TAACCCT program. TAACCCT provides community colleges and other eligible institutions of higher education with funds to expand and improve their ability to deliver education and career training programs that can be completed in 2 years or less, are suited for workers who are eligible for training under the TAA for Workers program, and prepare program participants for employment in high-wage, high-skill occupations. Through these multiyear grants, the Department of Labor is helping to ensure that our nation's institutions of higher education are helping adults succeed in acquiring the skills, degrees, and credentials needed for high-wage, high-skill employment while also meeting the needs of employers for skilled workers. The department is implementing the TAACCCT program in partnership with the Department of Education.

(Continued)

Table 8.2. Continued

Program, Website	Description
Workforce Innovation Fund https://innovation. workforcegps.org/about	The Workforce Innovation Fund Grant Program is authorized by the Full-Year Continuing Appropriations Act, 2011 (P.L. 112-10). These funds support innovative approaches to the design and delivery of employment and training services that generate long-term improvements in the performance of the public workforce system, both in terms of outcomes for job seekers and employer customers and cost-effectiveness. The program has the following goals: (a) provide services more efficiently to achieve better outcomes, particularly for vulnerable populations (e.g., low-wage and less skilled workers) and dislocated workers, especially those who have been unemployed for many months; (b) support both system reforms and innovations that facilitate cooperation across programs and funding streams in the delivery of client-centered services to job seekers, youth, and employers; and (c) emphasize building knowledge about effective practices through rigorous evaluation and translating "lessons learned" into improved labor market outcomes, the ability to bring such practices to scale in other geographic locations and increased cost efficiency in the broader workforce system.

Note: All program descriptions were excerpted from text downloaded from the referenced program site on October 23, 2015.

Not uncommonly, agency officials must make important policy decisions that entail trade-offs between the time needed to produce meaningful results, the breadth and depth of evidence on particular questions, and the salience of the issues to be studied. Indeed, a motivating factor for the conference that laid the groundwork for this *New Directions for Evaluation* issue was an interest in improving the evaluation tool kit and evaluation implementation to strengthen the capacity and proclivity of evaluators to expand the depth and breadth of questions they can reliably address within any evaluation. This includes, for example, designing evaluations that can more consistently inform questions about the intervention's effectiveness in different settings and with different population groups; the relative cost-effectiveness of policy or program design alternatives; projected effectiveness in different settings and contexts; "essential" ingredients for success; and reliable performance indicators of effectiveness and cost-effectiveness. To this end, the methods pursued include strategies that allow blending experimental analysis with non-experimental longitudinal observational analysis methods to improve the ability to extrapolate findings based on a time-limited experimental evaluation (Bell & Stuart, Chapter 3; St. Clair, Cook, & Hallberg, 2014).

Getting More out of Future Evaluations

A common theme in the preceding chapters of this issue is the quest to draw on the experiences of the past 40 years of policy and program evaluation to generate nuanced evaluation designs that support greater, more useful knowledge. In each chapter, the featured methodological "breakthrough" was motivated by the authors' recognition that the commonly used evaluation designs and strategies could be strengthened by some relatively easy-to-implement changes in how decisions are made about what to evaluate, when to evaluate, the optimal sample frame for the evaluation, and/or the analytic models used. An explicit or implicit motivation for expanding the methodological tool kit as described in these chapters was to add to what could be learned through a given evaluation. As the demand for evidence to inform policy continues to expand, it will be increasingly important for evaluators to be informed about the range and priority of questions that potentially could be addressed through a given study, considering both the immediate needs of the funding agency and prospective, complementary uses of the evidence. Armed with a better awareness of current and future needs for evidence and a stronger arsenal of methods, evaluators should proactively incorporate this information into study designs rather than merely make note of the "study limitations."

What constitutes valued information can vary widely. Some prospective consumers may want a simple "thumbs up" or "thumbs down" regarding the effectiveness of a particular program or policy, whereas others may be more interested in understanding how variation in implementation or context affects impacts. For example, the congressionally mandated evaluation of the Title V State Abstinence Education Grant program was commissioned to answer a politically charged question: Will moving from current practices of delivering health and sex education (which varied considerably across states and schools within states) to practices adhering to the strict definition of abstinence-only health and sex education set forth in the federal legislation lead to more or less sexual activity and sexual health risks for young people? (Trenholm et al., 2008). Agency staff and the research team also recognized the value of learning more about the variability in impacts across contexts and of advancing knowledge about the mechanisms through which change, if any, occurred. But, whatever was learned in these areas was considered "bonus" knowledge.

Similarly, the key question in the Head Start Impact Study was whether making Head Start available to 3- and 4-year olds would improve their readiness for Kindergarten (Puma, Bell, Cook, & Heid, 2010). Important secondary questions pertained to whether Head Start affected parental practices thought to be important for school readiness, the conditions under which services were effective, and which Head Start services were most important for improving child outcomes.

Both the Abstinence Education Grant Program Evaluation and the Head Start Impact Study were high-quality randomized controlled trials (see the Teen Pregnancy Prevention Evidence Review of the former and the What Works Clearinghouse reviewed studies database for the latter). Yet, both studies were able to address only a limited number of secondary questions of interest to policymakers. In the Abstinence Education Grant Program Evaluation, the priority was obtaining reliable estimates of the impacts of four well-defined programs with documentable counterfactuals, which ranged from very little formal health and sex education in one site to a fairly rich set of education and services, including instruction on contraceptive use, in other sites (Maynard et al., 2005). Although the study provided site-specific estimates of impacts, it was not designed to support rigorous exploration of questions about "for whom" and "under what conditions" the intervention might be effective. Moreover, the findings were not generalizable beyond the four programs that were studied.

In contrast, the Head Start Impact Study was designed to provide reliable estimates of the average impacts of the national Head Start Program. It is among the few randomized controlled trials that relied on a nationally representative sample. This design allowed rigorous exploration of the moderating effects of family and community factors. However, because of the sample dispersion, it was not practical for the evaluators to conduct an in-depth study of the conditions under which services were effective.

The next section of this chapter offers reflections about how future evaluations could be designed to be even more useful given advances in evaluation methods and improvements in data availability. These strategies include making trade-offs between precision of estimates for multiple

contexts and settings and expanding the reference contexts for impact estimates (Bell & Stuart, Chapter 3; Olsen & Orr, Chapter 4); blending experimental and nonexperimental methods for exploring the "black box"—for
whom and under what conditions interventions are effective (Bell & Peck,
Chapter 7; Bell & Stuart, Chapter 3); and using implementation evaluation
and performance assessments to gauge the relevance of impact evaluations
of particular programs, policies, or practices (Epstein & Klerman, Chapter
2; Mead, Chapter 5).

Strategies for Improving the Pace and Utility of Evaluation Research

Collectively, this chapter's authors have more than 60 years of experience
running programs, evaluating programs and policies, and translating evaluation findings for policymakers and program administrators. This experience spans the early days of the negative income tax experiments through
the present (Rossi & Lyall, 1976; Widerquist, 2005). Over this time, we have
seen major developments in the nature of public policies, in the policymaking processes, and in the availability of and reliance on evidence to inform
policy decisions and shape practice. Importantly, we also have seen major
improvements in the infrastructure to support policy analysis and program
evaluation, including increased attention to protection of human subjects
and data privacy. In particular, much more and better administrative data
are now available, with better systems linking data across systems and over
time for individuals and institutions and much greater capacity for creative
use of data to monitor program performance, assess the effectiveness and
comparative effectiveness of alternative policies and practices, simulate the
expected impacts of policy changes, and more generally to support scientific
inquiry (Chowdry, Crawford, Dearden, Goodman, & Vignoles, 2013; Figlio,
Karbownik, & Salvanes, 2015; Manzi, 2012; Rolston, Chapter 1; Tang, Agarwal, O'Brien, & Meyer, 2010). At the same time, the regulations governing
access to those data have increased in complexity (see, e.g., the Privacy and
Technical Assistance Center at the U.S. Department of Education; data access policies at the Bureau of Labor Statistics; and the health information
privacy policies and the ACF Confidentiality Toolkit at the U.S. Department
of Health and Human Services).

In tandem with advances in the quality and accessibility of administrative data systems, we also have witnessed the development of a robust
social science "research industry" with staffs of highly skilled statisticians,
econometricians, and other social scientists whose academic training has
prepared them to design and carry out complex multimethod policy analyses and program evaluations (Gueron & Rolston, 2013). Innovative strategies for addressing some of the common shortcomings of program evaluations have emerged from the insightful pairing of advances in applied
statistics with the recognized limitations of previous program evaluations

for informing a broader range of questions than commonly included in the formal evaluation plan.

In the remainder of this chapter, we draw on our experiences leading evaluation agencies within the federal government to suggest ways that the evaluation community might integrate these and other strategies into their work to better serve decision makers' immediate and longer term needs. A common thread is the importance of more and better communication between the evaluation and policy community regarding the policy context currently and into the future, and the implications of contexts for decisions about what is to be evaluated, how evaluations should be conducted, and how best to communicate the findings of the evaluations.

Invest in Understanding the Broad Context for Evaluation

The usefulness of evaluations could be improved by grounding them in a deep understanding of the underlying policy concerns and context. Good evaluation planning requires understanding the policy concerns, which often are masked by a generic descriptor, such as teen pregnancy, career readiness, or achievement gaps. For example, there are many reasons to be concerned about teenage pregnancy, some related to the circumstances of the pregnancy (e.g., voluntary or not, intentionality, and context), some related to consequences for the mother and/or her child (e.g., economic, school status, and child welfare), and others related to public welfare (e.g., social service costs and economic growth). The optimal evaluation design could vary accordingly, even though it would be valuable to squeeze out of any evaluation of teenage pregnancy prevention information relevant to all perspectives.

The challenge is establishing efficient, collegial mechanisms for evaluators to gain the necessary foundational knowledge required to come up with an optimal study design. The optimal design is one that not only returns highly credible evidence on the most pressing questions of the sponsor but also anticipates secondary concerns of the sponsor and other interested parties. A very useful strategy for this purpose is to invest in the development of program and evaluation logic models, typically with considerable input from policymaker and practitioner stakeholders about the underlying assumptions that are guiding policy or practice decisions (W. K. Kellogg Foundation, 2004). Such a logic model provides a template for explicitly stating what aspects of that logic will be informed (and how) through the evaluation.

Some of the most useful federal evaluations have relied on well-crafted logic models to guide the study design. As a result, the findings provided both overall evidence of the program or policy effectiveness and an understanding of where the underlying assumptions that guided the policy or program were or were not supported by the evidence. For example, the Building Strong Families Demonstration tackled a very challenging policy concern: the large number of children being born to unmarried couples whose economic and social circumstances were fragile and who had high probabilities of poor health, education, and economic outcomes. By designing an evaluation that was closely aligned with the program logic, the evaluation was able not only to examine outcomes for the children born into such families but also program inputs and outputs (such as participation) and intermediate outcomes such as the parents' relationship quality and stability (Carlson, McLanahan, England, & Devaney, 2005; Wood, McConnell, Moore, Clarkwest, & Hseuh, 2012; Wood, Moore, Clarkwest, Killewald, & Monahan, 2012).

Design Evaluations with a Neutral View of What the Outcome Might Be

Generally, evaluations focus on programs and policies that are intended as solutions to particular problems. In response, the expectation is that the impacts will be favorable. This emphasis favors being prepared for replication, assuming a policy or practice is shown to be effective, over understanding why the strategy might not have worked as planned, should the evaluation not demonstrate evidence of effectiveness. What this means in practice is that the evaluations tend to be better able to generate evidence in support of the underlying assumptions than on advancing our understanding of why those underlying assumptions may not have held.

Calculations by the study authors of data in the Reviewed Studies Database (Institute of Education Sciences, 2015) indicate that only about 10% of the single-study reviews conducted by the What Works Clearinghouse that met evidence standards without reservations reported statistically significant impact findings. This rate is comparable to the proportion of drug trials that moved from Phase 1 to U.S. Food and Drug Administration approval over a 9-year period beginning in 2002—also 10% (Hay, Thomas, Craighead, Economides, & Rosenthal, 2014). Insofar as null findings are much more common than favorable findings, it is important to design studies so that they can help explain all findings, regardless what they are.

The recommendations put forth by Epstein and Klerman in Chapter 2 would likely increase the "success" rate for program and policy evaluations by reducing the number of summative evaluations (i.e., evaluations that aim to estimate the effectiveness expected under conditions of normal practice) that are launched before the policies have been implemented with adequate fidelity. These recommendations would be especially helpful in designing effectiveness studies (i.e., summative evaluations) under the tiered framework for evaluation designs, such as that put forth recently by the National Science Foundation and the U.S. Department of Education (Earle, Maynard, & Neild, 2013). This framework also would be easily adaptable for incorporating the guidance for performance analysis proposed by Mead in Chapter 5.

Bend the Rules of Optimal Evaluation When Warranted to Balance Competing Priorities

In some cases, there may be benefits to "breaking the rules" about good evaluations. Two such rules that sometimes warrant breaking, or bending, pertain to fidelity of implementation and stability of implementation. There is a role in the policy development process for evidence on the efficacy of strategies under ideal circumstances, as well as for evidence on the effectiveness of strategies as they are likely to be implemented (i.e., under conditions of normal practice). Epstein and Klerman (Chapter 2) provide a compelling case for circumstances under which one might want to defer evaluation until implementation fidelity has been achieved—circumstances in which the goal is to learn whether a scripted policy or practice will work. This recommendation is well aligned with the normal design-based intervention research model (Fishman, 2014; Fishman, Penuel, Allen, Cheng, & Sabelli, 2013). However, there are other conditions in which policymakers need evidence about effects under conditions of routine practice—for example, when the government issues the script but others have responsibility for implementation and monitoring.

It also can be very useful to relax this rule when we are in pursuit of marginal improvements in policies or practices. For example, there can be great advantages to "tinkering" with things such as the frequency or mode of income verification for program eligibility, program eligibility requirements or referral protocols, or the regulations governing how specific federal resources, such as special education funds, can be used. There also can be advantages to learning from field-initiated interventions targeted at particular problems, such as pregnancy prevention or school dropout prevention. On the one hand, evaluating programs or policies that have not yet been implemented with fidelity may lead to failures to identify some potentially successful strategies. On the other hand, pushing for implementation fidelity before conducting serious evaluations may accelerate innovation and evidence generation—and the timing of evidence is important for relevance to the policy process.

Given the length of time needed to answer some evaluation questions and the comparatively rapid pace of change in the political and policy environment, evaluation funders cannot count on being able to follow a planned sequence of studies. Rather, in planning a major, long-term evaluation, it may be wise to exercise one's best judgment as to whether an efficacy approach or an effectiveness approach will be most useful. In many cases, there may not be a second chance to demonstrate effectiveness.

Another reason to break the rules is when interim evaluation findings suggest possible implementation weaknesses and/or evaluation design

NEW DIRECTIONS FOR EVALUATION • DOI: 10.1002/ev

limitations that could be addressed midstream. For example, in a field test of welfare policy changes aimed at improving school completion and work readiness of teenage mothers, evaluators noted early on that a critical feature of the federal policy change—the sanction policy for noncompliance with participation requirements—was not being implemented by the local field staff. This lack of fidelity quite likely would have gone unnoticed had there not been a large-scale evaluation of the policy change taking place. However, in this case, early implementation research findings prompted the federal oversight team to "retrain" the local field staff and monitor their compliance with requirements that they reduce the grants of women who failed to meet the mandated requirements for school attendance and/or employment (Hershey, Nagatoshi, & Polit, 1989; Maynard, 1993). The evaluation continued, with the study team "marking" the data for the date of the midcourse correction. This allowed a fairer test of the intended policy as well as some practical lessons about how to structure federal guidance and oversight for scale-up, should the program be institutionalized.

A demonstration of paraprofessional home visiting services for teenage parents offers a parallel experience. In this study, the evaluators noted that recipients of the home visits were experiencing very high rates of repeat pregnancies. This was despite indications from surveys that the recipients did not desire to have another child in the near term and administrative data indicating that home visitors had been completing the expected conversations with the teenage mothers regarding their family planning goals and access to services. Armed with information from the evaluation, the program staff conducted a performance analysis and concluded that it should retrain staff and implement a new strategy for home visit monitoring to allow more immediate professional development through supervisor modelling in cases where deviations from best practice were observed. (In this case, although case workers were covering the family planning topics prescribed by the program, they were not especially comfortable with or effective in their delivery.) By marking the evaluation data with the date of the policy change, it was possible to examine experiences before and after the programmatic change (Kelsey, Johnson, & Maynard, 2001).

Use the Ideal to Guide the Path to a Constrained Optimal Evaluation Design

Coming up with optimal evaluation designs entails balancing the ideal with practical considerations, as well as the interests of multiple audiences. Colleagues on the front line of policy development rely on policy analysts and evaluation staff to provide credible, contextualized guidance about what is and is not known to support various options in terms of effectiveness, burden, and risks. There certainly is value in extending a core experimental impact evaluation to include complementary low-cost add-ons (e.g., conducting a blended experimental and quasi-experimental design to extend the generalizability of the study findings, as suggested by Bell and Stuart (Chapter 3); using endogenous subgroup analytic techniques as proposed by Peck (Chapter 6), or simulation analysis, as suggested by Olsen and Orr (Chapter 4) to extend the analysis beyond questions that can be answered using the experimental design). However, it is important to carefully weigh the expected returns to each add-on relative to the costs.

In many instances, it may be most effective to reserve some resources during the initial design phase of a project to be allocated later in response to emergent findings. For example, such reserve funds might be best spent on having the evaluation team work in tandem with the program team to investigate a serious implementation problem identified during the study, such as high program attrition. In the case of the Teenage Parent Home Visitor Demonstration Evaluation noted previously, funds were needed to investigate plausible reasons for high repeat pregnancy rates and to support "corrective measures" by the program staff.

Consider Integrating Opportunities for Midcourse Corrections into the Evaluation

"Rapid-cycle evaluations" have gained recent attention and offer a way to produce more timely evaluation results that can identify opportunities for midcourse corrections (Bryk et al., 2015; Cohen-Vogel et al., 2015; Hannan, Russell, Takahashi, & Park, 2015; Urban, Hargraves, & Trochim, 2014; Vaishnavi & Kuechler, 2015). Rapid-cycle evaluations typically examine outputs or near-term outcomes that can be achieved and measured quickly, often using administrative data that will be collected in any event and that can be used at minimal additional cost. Drawing on strong logic models, as described earlier, a rapid-cycle evaluation can be constructed to test for impacts on implementation elements, allowing corrective action to ensure that the ultimate impact evaluation will reflect strong implementation. For example, a program providing coaching to teachers in hopes of improving student outcomes might measure teacher participation in the coaching and build in interim tests for improvements in teacher skills or behavior. Rapid-cycle evaluations also can be conducted independently when short-term outputs or outcomes are of inherent interest.

Have a Strong Plan for Disseminating Evaluation Findings

An emerging body of evidence examines the ways and extent to which evaluation findings do or do not influence policy and practice (Humphries, Stafinski, Mumtaz, & Menon, 2014; Oliver et al., 2014; Tseng & Nutley, 2014). Recognizing that evaluation findings may be useful to many audiences, it is important to plan for dissemination from the beginning of an evaluation study. Evaluation funders may even require a dissemination plan as part of the competitive bidding process. Identifying and prioritizing audiences for the evaluation early can help evaluators refine the evaluation questions and develop well-balanced analysis plans. Engaging desired audiences along the way, for example, through a newsletter describing the study's progress, can promote interest and understanding of findings when they become available.

Several federal online libraries of literature about research and evaluation and programmatic experience have been developed with the explicit intent to serve as a resource for practitioners to share and learn about emerging evaluations and operational lessons. The Workforce Strategies Solutions at the U.S. Department of Labor and the Self-Sufficiency Research Clearinghouse operated by the Administration for Children and Families at the U.S. Department of Health and Human Services (HHS) are examples of such registries of information and findings. These differ from the evidence-based clearinghouses in that they do not rate the quality of the methodology or results beyond establishing minimum standards for inclusion.

Increasingly, funders and journals are also promoting openness by requiring or encouraging evaluators to preregister analysis plans at publicly available sites such as ClinicalTrials.gov (see https://clinicaltrials.gov/), the American Economic Association's Social Science Registry (see http://socialscienceregistry.org/), and the Open Science Framework (see https://osf.io/).

Two important benefits of even simple clearinghouses of program and policy evaluations are: (a) providing ready access to information about programs and policies that have been or are currently being evaluated including a link to information about the progress and/or findings to date; and (b) offering a basis for identifying evaluations that were started but for which results were never reported. Indeed, a robust body of literature documents the pervasive "file-drawer" problem in intervention research (Franco, Malhotra, & Simonovits, 2014; Ioannidis, Munafo, Fussar-Poli, Nosek, & David, 2014; Maynard, Vaughn, Sarteschi, & Berglundet, 2014; Pigott, Valentine, Polanin, & Williams, 2013).

A seemingly simple solution to this problem is to insist on comprehensive reporting of design, methods, and results. Indeed, both the U.S. Department of Labor and the Administration for Children and Families at HHS have evaluation policies that require this (see, e.g., U.S. Department of Health and Human Services, 2012; U.S. Department of Labor, 2014).

Thorough reporting ensures transparency, allowing well-informed critiques and supporting replication. Such reporting is a hallmark of federally sponsored evaluations. However, such dense, heavy, lengthy reports are attractive primarily to research and evaluation audiences. Policymakers, practitioners, advocates, and others are typically more interested in shorter products highlighting major findings or focusing on specific topics within the broader evaluation. Developing multiple products in different formats requires time and money but is one more way to make the most of our evaluation investments.

Conclusions

The field of program evaluation has matured tremendously in the United States in the past 4 decades. It is now commonly understood that rigorous impact evaluations are critical, with a strong emphasis on using experimental designs to the maximum extent possible. The empirical superiority of experimental designs is well understood by most federal officials, who have become accustomed to large-scale evaluations as well as smaller, rapid, and iterative evaluations. Several challenges must still be addressed, however. One priority should be to adopt sophisticated designs to address generalizability, without compromising the empirical rigor of impact evaluations. There also is an ongoing need to balance the empirical "rules" of experimental evaluations, particularly as related to long-term impacts, with the need of both policymakers and administrators for more timely evidence and the need of program operators to understand and translate evaluation findings to improve program service delivery and implementation. The chapters in this issue present compelling approaches that represent the "next generation" of high-quality human services evaluations.

Disclaimer

The views expressed in this chapter are those of the authors and do not represent positions of the federal government, the U.S. Department of Health and Human Services, the U.S. Department of Labor, or the U.S. Department of Education.

References

Bryk, A. S. (2009). Support a science of performance improvement. *Phi Delta Kappan*, *90*, 597–600.

Bryk, A. S., Gomez, L. M., Grunow, A., & LeMahieu, P. G. (2015). *Learning to improve: How America's schools can get better at getting better*. Cambridge, MA: Harvard University Press.

Butler, D., Alson, J., Bloom, D., Deitch, V., Hill, A., Hsueh, ... Redcross, C. (2012). *What strategies work for the hard-to-employ? Final Results of the Hard-to-Employ Demonstration and Evaluation Project and selected sites from the Employment Retention and Advancement Project* (OPRE Report No. 2012-08). Washington, DC: U.S. Department of Health and Human Services, Administration for Children and Families, Office of Planning, Research and Evaluation.

Carlson, M., McLanahan, S., England, P., & Devaney, B. (2005). *What we know about unmarried parents: Implications for building strong families programs* (Building Strong Families Brief No. 3). Princeton, NJ: Mathematica Policy Research.

Chowdry, H., Crawford, C., Dearden, L., Goodman, A., & Vignoles, A. (2013). Widening participation in higher education: Analysis using linked administrative Data. *Journal of the Royal Statistical Society: Series A, 176*, 431–457.

Cohen-Vogel, L., Tichnor-Wagner, A., Allen, D., Harrison, C., Kainz, K., Socol, A. R., & Wang, Q. (2015). Implementing educational innovations at scale: Transforming researchers into continuous improvement scientists. *Educational Policy, 29*, 257–277.

Daly, A. J., Finnigan, K. S., Moolenaar, N. M., & Che, J. (2014). The critical role of brokers in the access and use of evidence at the school and district level. In K. S. Finnigan & A. J. Daly (Eds.), *Using research evidence in education* (pp. 13–31). Cham, Switzerland: Springer International Publishing.

Durlak, J. A., & DuPre, E. P. (2008). Implementation matters: A review of research on the influence of implementation on program outcomes and the factors affecting implementation. *American Journal of Community Psychology, 41*, 327–350.

Earle, J., Maynard, R., & Neild, R. (2013). *Common evidence guidelines for education research.* Washington, DC: Institute of Education Sciences and National Science Foundation. Retrieved from http://ies.ed.gov/pdf/CommonGuidelines.pdf

Figlio, D. N., Karbownik, K., & Salvanes, K. G. (2015). *Education research and administrative data* (NBER Working Paper No. w21592). Cambridge, MA: National Bureau of Economic Research.

Fishman, B. J. (2014). Designing usable interventions: Bringing student perspectives to the table. *Instructional Science, 42*, 115–121.

Fishman, B. J., Penuel, W. R., Allen, A. R., Cheng, B. H., & Sabelli, N. (2013). Design-based implementation research: An emerging model for transforming the relationship of research and practice. In B. J. Fishman & W. R. Penuel (Eds.), *National Society for the Study of Education: Vol 112. Design based implementation research* (pp. 136–156).

Fixsen, D. L., Naoom, S. F., Blase, K. A., Friedman, R. M., & Wallace, F. (2005). *Implementation research: A synthesis of the literature* (FMHI Publication No. 231). Tampa, FL: University of South Florida, Louis de la Parte Florida Mental Health Institute, The National Implementation Research Network. Retrieved from http://nirn.fpg.unc.edu/sites/nirn.fpg.unc.edu/files/resources/NIRN-MonographFull-01-2005.pdf

Franco, A., Malhotra, N., & Simonovits, G. (2014). Publication bias in the social sciences: Unlocking the file drawer. *Science, 345*, 1502–1505.

Granger, R. C., & Maynard, R. (2015). Unlocking the potential of the "what works" approach to policymaking and practice improving impact evaluations. *American Journal of Evaluation, 34*, 558–549. doi:1098214015594420

Gueron, J., & Rolston, H. (2013). *Fighting for reliable evidence.* New York: Russell Sage Foundation.

Hannan, M., Russell, J. L., Takahashi, S., & Park, S. (2015). Using improvement science to better support beginning teachers: The case of the Building a Teaching Effectiveness Network. *Journal of Teacher Education, 66*, 494–508.

Haskins, R., & Baron, J. (2011). *Building the connection between policy and evidence.* London, UK: NESTA. Retrieved from http://coalition4evidence.org/wp-content/uploads/uploads-dupes-safety/Haskins-Baron-paper-on-fed-evid-based-initiatives-2011.pdf

Haskins, R., & Margolis, G. (2014). *Show me the evidence: Obama's fight for rigor and results in social policy.* Washington, DC: Brookings.

Hay, M., Thomas, D. W., Craighead, J. L., Economides, C., & Rosenthal, J. (2014). Clinical development success rates for investigational drugs. *Nature Biotechnology, 32*, 40–51.

Hershey, A., Nagatoshi, C., & Polit, D. (1989). *Implementing services for welfare dependent teenage parents: Experiences in the DHHS/OFA Teenage Parent Demonstration.* Princeton, NJ: Mathematica Policy Research.

Humphries, S., Stafinski, T., Mumtaz, Z., & Menon, D. (2014). Barriers and facilitators to evidence-use in program management: A systematic review of the literature. *BMC Health Services Research, 14*, 171.

Institute of Education Sciences, National Center for Education Evaluation. (2015). *What Works Clearinghouse, Study findings data base.* Retrieved from http://ies.ed.gov/ncee/wwc/StudyFindings.aspx

Ioannidis, J. P., Munafo, M. R., Fusar-Poli, P., Nosek, B. A., & David, S. P. (2014). Publication and other reporting biases in cognitive sciences: Detection, prevalence, and prevention. *Trends in Cognitive Sciences, 18*, 235–241.

Kelsey, M., Johnson, A., & Maynard, R. (2001). *The potential of home visitor services to strengthen welfare-to-work programs for teenage parents on cash assistance.* University of Pennsylvania and Mathematica Policy Research. Retrieved from http://www.mathematica-mpr.com/~/media/publications/pdfs/potential.pdf

Kemple, J. J., & Willner, C. J. (2008). *Career Academies long-term impacts on labor market outcomes, educational attainment, and transitions to adulthood.* New York: MDRC.

Manzi, J. (2012). *Uncontrolled: The surprising payoff of trial-and-error for business, politics, and society.* New York: Basic Books.

Maynard, B. S., Vaughn, M. G., Sarteschi, C. M., & Berglundet, A. H. (2014). Social work dissertation research: Contributing to scholarly discourse or the file drawer? *British Journal of Social Work, 44*, 1045–1062.

Maynard, R. A. (1993). *Building self-sufficiency among welfare-dependent teenage parents.* Princeton, NJ: Mathematica Policy Research. Retrieved from http://aspe.hhs.gov/execsum/building-self-sufficiency-among-welfare-dependent-teenage-parents

Maynard, R. A., Trenholm, C., Devaney, B., Johnson, A., Clark, M. A., Homrighausen, J., & Kalay, E. (2005). *First-year impacts of four Title V, Section 510 abstinence education programs.* Princeton, NJ: Mathematica Policy Research.

Mervis, J. (2013). An invisible hand behind plan to realign U.S. science education. *Science, 3412*, 338–341. Retrieved from http://portal.scienceintheclassroom.org/sites/default/files/post-files/science-2013-mervis-338-41.pdf

Murnane, R. J., & Willett, J. B. (2010). *Methods matter: Improving causal inference in educational and social science research.* Oxford, UK: Oxford University Press.

Nussle, J., & Orszag, P. (Eds.). (2014). *Moneyball for government.* Washington, DC: Disruption Books.

Nutley, S., Davies, H., & Walter, I. (2002). *Evidence based policy and practice: Cross sector lessons from the UK* (Working Paper No. 9). London, UK: ESRC UK Centre for Evidence Based Policy and Practice.

Oates, J. (2012, May 7). Reemployment Eligibility Assessments (REAs) [Web log post]. U.S. Department of Labor Blog. Retrieved from http://blog.dol.gov/2012/05/07/reemployment-eligibility-assessments-reas/

Oliver, K., Innvar, S., Lorenc, T., Woodman, J., & Thomas, J. (2014). A systematic review of barriers to and facilitators of the use of evidence by policymakers. *BMC Health Services Research, 14*, 2.

Orr, L. L. (1999). *Social experiments: Evaluating public programs with experimental methods.* Thousand Oaks, CA: Sage Publications.

Pigott, T. D., Valentine, J. C., Polanin, J. R., & Williams, R. T. (2013). Outcome-reporting bias in education research. *Educational Researcher, 2*, 424–432.

Poe-Yamagata, E., Benus, J., Bill, N., Carrington, H., Michaelides, M., & Shen, T. (2011). *Impact of the Reemployment and Eligibility Assessment Initiative.* Columbia, MD: IMPAQ International.

Puma, M., Bell, S., Cook, R., & Heid, C., with Shapiro, G., Broene, P., ... Spier, E. (2010). *Head Start Impact Study: Final report.* Washington, DC: U.S. Department of Health and Human Services, Administration for Children & Families.

Rossi, P. H., & Lyall, K. C. (1976). *Reforming public welfare: A critique of the Negative Income Tax Experiment.* New York: Russell Sage Foundation.

Schochet, P. Z., Burghardt, J., & McConnell, S. (2008). Does Job Corps work? Impact findings from the National Job Corps Study. *American Economic Review, 98*, 1864–1886.

St. Clair, T., Cook, T. D., & Hallberg, K. (2014). Examining the internal validity and statistical precision of the comparative interrupted time series design by comparison with a randomized experiment. *American Journal of Evaluation, 35,* 311–317. doi:1098214014527337

Tang, D., Agarwal, A., O'Brien, D., & Meyer, M. (2010). Overlapping experiment infrastructure: More, better, faster experimentation. In *Proceedings of the 16th Conference on Knowledge Discovery and Data Mining,* Washington, DC (pp. 17–26). New York: Association for Computing Machinery. doi:10.1145/1835804.1835810

Trenholm, C., Devaney, B., Fortson, K., Clark, M., Quay, L., & Wheeler, J. (2008). Impacts of abstinence education on teen sexual activity, risk of pregnancy, and risk of sexually transmitted diseases. *Journal of Policy Analysis and Management, 27,* 255–276.

Tseng, V. (2012). The uses of research in policy and practice. *Social Policy Report, 26*(2). Retrieved from http://www.srcd.org/sites/default/files/documents/spr_262_fiinal.pdf

Tseng, V. (2014). Forging common ground: Fostering the conditions for evidence use. *Journal of Leisure Research, 46,* 6.

Tseng, V., & Nutley, S. (2014). Building the infrastructure to improve the use and usefulness of research in education. In K. S. Finnigan & A. J. Daly (Eds.), *Using research evidence in education* (pp. 163–175). Cham, Switzerland: Springer International Publishing.

U.S. Department of Education. (2014). Applications for new awards, Performance Partnership Pilots. *Federal Register,* November 24, 70033;ln70051. Retrieved from https://federalregister.gov/a/2014-27775

U.S. Department of Education. (2015). Final priority, Investing in Education. *Federal Register,* June 5, pp. 32210–32215. Retrieved from https://www.federalregister.gov/articles/2015/06/05/2015-13671/final-priority-investing-in-innovation-fund

U.S. Department of Health and Human Services. (2012). *ACF evaluation policy.* Washington, DC: Author. Retrieved from http://www.acf.hhs.gov/programs/opre/resource/acf-evaluation-policy

U.S. Department of Labor. (2014). *Department of Labor evaluation policy.* Washington, DC: Author. Retrieved from http://www.dol.gov/asp/evaluation/EvaluationPolicy.html

U.S. Department of Labor. (2015). *Trade Adjustment Assistance Community College and Career Training Grant Program (TAACCCT).* Washington, DC: Author. Retrieved from http://doleta.gov/taaccct/pdf/TAACCCT_One_Pagers_All.pdf

Urban, J. B., Hargraves, M., & Trochim, W. M. (2014). Evolutionary evaluation: Implications for evaluators, researchers, practitioners, funders and the evidence-based program mandate. *Evaluation and Program Planning, 45,* 127–139.

Vaishnavi, V. K., & Kuechler, W. (2015). *Design science research methods and patterns: Innovating information and communication technology.* Boca Raton, FL: CRC Press.

W.K. Kellogg Foundation. (2004). *Logic model development guide.* Battle Creek, MI: Author. Retrieved from http://www.wkkf.org/resource-directory/resource/2006/02/wk-kellogg-foundation-logic-model-development-guide

Weiss, M., Bloom, H., & Brock, T. (2014). A conceptual framework for studying the sources of variation in program effects. *Journal of Policy Analysis and Management, 33,* 778–808.

Widerquist, K. (2005). A failure to communicate: What (if anything) can we learn from the negative income tax experiments? *Journal of Socio-Economics, 34,* 49–81.

Wood, R. G., McConnell, S., Moore, Q., Clarkwest, A., & Hsueh, J. (2012). The effects of Building Strong Families: A healthy marriage and relationship skills education program for unmarried parents. *Journal of Policy Analysis and Management, 31,* 228–252.

Wood, R. G., Moore, Q., Clarkwest, A., Killewald, A., & Monahan, S. (2012). *The long-term effects of Building Strong Families: A relationship skills education program for unmarried parents.* Princeton, NJ: Mathematica Policy Research.

REBECCA MAYNARD is University Trustee Professor of Education and Social Policy, University of Pennsylvania.

NAOMI GOLDSTEIN is deputy assistant secretary for planning, research, and evaluation at the Administration for Children and Families, U.S. Department of Health and Human Services.

DEMETRA SMITH NIGHTINGALE is the chief evaluation officer at the U.S. Department of Labor.

NEW DIRECTIONS FOR EVALUATION • DOI: 10.1002/ev

INDEX

137

Title V State Abstinence Education Grant program, 123
Tough, P., 80
Trade Adjustment Act Community College Career Training Program (TAAC-CCT), 114, 120
Traeger, L., 67
Trenholm, C., 123
Trochim, W. M., 129
Tseng, V., 112, 115, 129
Turner, M. A., 92

Unlu, F., 88
Urban, J. B., 129
U.S. Department of Health and Human Services (USDHHS), 100

Vaden-Kiernan, M., 48, 64
Vaishnavi, V. K., 129
Valentine, J. C., 130
Van de Ven, A. H., 80
Vaughn, M. G., 130
Victor, T., 11
Vignoles, A., 124

Wallace, F., 110
Walter, I., 112, 115
Walter, J., 76, 98, 99
Wandersman, A., 38

Wang, Q., 129
Weaver, R. K., 81
Weingardt, K. R., 48
Weiss, C. H., 79
Weiss, M., 110
Werner, A., 98, 100
West, M. R., 89
What Works Clearinghouse, 62–63, 116
Wheeler, J., 123
Whitman, D., 80
Wholey, J. S., 13, 35, 75
Widerquist, K., 124
Wildavsky, A., 74
Willett, J. B., 110
Williams, R. T., 130
Willner, C. J., 116, 118
Wiseman, M., 48, 79
Wong, V. C., 9, 52
Wood, M., 98, 126
Woodman, J., 112, 129
Wood, R. G., 126
Work force Innovation Fund, 114
Work Incentive (WIN) program, 76

Yoshikawa, H., 79

Zedlewski, S. R., 75
Zhu, P., 88

NEW DIRECTIONS FOR EVALUATION

ORDER FORM SUBSCRIPTION AND SINGLE ISSUES

DISCOUNTED BACK ISSUES:

Use this form to receive 20% off all back issues of *New Directions for Evaluation*.
All single issues priced at **$23.20** (normally $29.00)

TITLE	ISSUE NO.	ISBN

Call 1-800-835-6770 or see mailing instructions below. When calling, mention the promotional code JBNND to receive your discount. For a complete list of issues, please visit www.wiley.com/WileyCDA/WileyTitle/productCd-EV.html

SUBSCRIPTIONS: (1 YEAR, 4 ISSUES)

☐ New Order   ☐ Renewal

U.S.	☐ Individual: $89	☐ Institutional: $380
CANADA/MEXICO	☐ Individual: $89	☐ Institutional: $422
ALL OTHERS	☐ Individual: $113	☐ Institutional: $458

Call 1-800-835-6770 or see mailing and pricing instructions below.
Online subscriptions are available at www.onlinelibrary.wiley.com

ORDER TOTALS:

Issue / Subscription Amount: $ _____

Shipping Amount: $ _____
(for single issues only – subscription prices include shipping)

Total Amount: $ _____

SHIPPING CHARGES:	
First Item	$6.00
Each Add'l Item	$2.00

(No sales tax for U.S. subscriptions. Canadian residents, add GST for subscription orders. Individual rate subscriptions must be paid by personal check or credit card. Individual rate subscriptions may not be resold as library copies.)

BILLING & SHIPPING INFORMATION:

☐ **PAYMENT ENCLOSED:** *(U.S. check or money order only. All payments must be in U.S. dollars.)*

☐ **CREDIT CARD:** ☐ VISA ☐ MC ☐ AMEX

Card number _____ Exp. Date_____

Card Holder Name_____ Card Issue # _____

Signature _____ Day Phone_____

☐ **BILL ME:** *(U.S. institutional orders only. Purchase order required.)*

Purchase order # _____
Federal Tax ID 13559302 • GST 89102-8052

Name _____

Address_____

Phone_____ E-mail_____

Copy or detach page and send to: **John Wiley & Sons, Inc. / Jossey Bass**
PO Box 55381
Boston, MA 02205-9850

PROMO JBNND